ADVOCACY FOR THE ADVOCATE

To my Secretary

ADVOCACY FOR THE ADVOCATE

Second Edition

ERIC CROWTHER, OBE

Former London Stipendiary Magistrate; a Recorder of the South-Eastern Circuit;
Lecturer on Advocacy for the Council of Legal Education 1955–1988;
Chairman of the Training Sub-Committee of the Inner London Magistrates' Courts Service 1981–1989

ISBN 0 85121 672 2

First Edition 1984
Second Edition 1990

Published by
Longman Law, Tax and Finance
Longman Group UK Ltd
24–27 Lamb's Conduit Street
London WC1N 3NJ

Associated Offices
Australia, Hong Kong, Malaysia, Singapore, USA

A CIP catalogue record for this book is available from the British Library

Printed and bound in Great Britain by
Biddles Ltd, Guildford and King's Lynn

Contents

Foreword to the first edition

This is a most refreshing book. It is full of entertainment as well as wisdom. The human face (warts and all) of the law in action is revealed to us by one who loves it. But our author is not content merely to entertain. He has a serious purpose: by telling the truth of what happens in court he is concerned to improve the quality of advocacy.

Advocacy is an art, not a science. It requires a penetrating insight into the strengths and weaknesses of man and woman, a passion for justice, and the will to fight for it. Experience, character, and mature talent are the winning combination.

Eric Crowther is himself no ordinary advocate. He has the gift of a persuasive tongue, a wide experience of mankind, and the passion for justice. Fortunately, he can also write with wit as well as insight. He calls the book 'Advocacy for the Advocate', and so in a very real sense it is. But it is more. He describes in a way which all can enjoy and understand the practice of advocacy in those courts which really matter—to the citizen—the magistrates' court, the county court, and the Crown Court.

In these courts no amount of legal learning will make a successful advocate. The nature of the art is persuasion. Yet it is this which troubles many people. Is advocacy fair?

Why should an advocate be able by the exercise of his skill to influence a court decision? Why should I (a disappointed client may say) lose because my barrister was not as good as the other man's?

If we were all able to explain the strong points in our case and to expose the weaknesses in the case for the other side, there would be no need for the professional advocate. But we are not. Advocacy is, therefore, a necessity if courts are to reach just decisions. Of course, it is a skill which can be abused. However there are safeguards. The courts and the governing bodies of the legal professions set the standards of integrity which are needed and they have the 'know-how' and experience to ensure that they are observed. The bully, or the sharp practitioner who conceals the truth or prostitutes the art, is soon shown up for what he is, and sooner or later, pays the penalty—which can be as severe as disqualification from his profession.

The importance of fair and skilful advocacy cannot be too strongly emphasised. Our system of justice depends upon it. The British legal system relies on the parties to produce the evidence and argument to enable the court to reach a just decision. Our courts are not inquisitors conducting their own independent investigation but deciders of questions put before them by the parties to the case. Good advocates (on both sides) are, therefore, indispensable. Indeed this is why we provide public moneys for the legal aid and assistance of litigants who have not the resources to pay a lawyer. And this is why there is a persistent demand for raising the financial limits within which legal aid is available.

Beneath, therefore, the laughter and tears of the court stories, which our author tells so enthusiastically, there lies a fundamental fact which few people really understand. The competent and honourable advocate is the workhorse of the system. The mills of justice grind slowly; but without the advocate they will not grind 'exceeding sure', and will be in peril of grinding to a halt.

Scarman
1984

Preface to the second edition

The law reflects life, and life is represented in the courts by advocacy. Life in this country has changed a lot in the six years since this book was first produced, and the reaction of the publishers to the changes in the law which have resulted has been to request a second edition of *Advocacy for the Advocate.*

The main change, for better or worse, in our system has been the advent of the Crown Prosecution Service, so I have included a chapter on the work of that not universally popular body. The advocate needs to be familiar with these changes in the law. Anyone appearing in a criminal case now needs to study carefully the Police and Criminal Evidence Act 1984, especially ss 76 and 78. The Criminal Justice Act 1988 introduced new provisions on bail and also restrictions on the award of custodial sentences, especially for offenders under twenty-one. The advocate's primary duties of integrity and honesty towards the court have been reinforced by the decisions in *Bridgwood* in 1988, both in the Crown Court, where the solicitor received a suspended prison sentence, and before the Solicitors' Disciplinary Tribunal, which fined him. These verdicts have far-reaching implications for advocates who know of a defendant's bad record when the CPS puts him or her forward as a person of good character.

Now that I have retired from being a stipendiary magistrate I have felt able to make the book a little racier, more robust, in places. And anyone who is thinking of presenting me with that tree mentioned in the Preface to the first edition should first read the introduction to my other book, *Last in the List,* which was published in 1988. I don't want to plant any more trees!

Eric Crowther
1990

Preface to the first edition

An Eastern philosopher said that there are three things that a man must do in his life: he must have a son, write a book, and plant a tree. Taking the Biblical span of three score years and ten as a life-time, I was more than half-way through it when I (or, more accurately, my wife) had a son, and he will have reached the age of majority (under the old as well as the new law) before this, my first, book is published. What about that tree? I have never been very interested in horticulture—indeed I have only done one day's gardening in my life. That was in America, when, as a student, I ran very short of money and worked in the immense New York garden of a very rich lady (I am afraid illegally) but succeeded only in breaking her electric mower and being sent away without the two dollars that I thought I had earned and with a threat of legal proceedings in respect of the broken machine. So if anyone is anxious to help me fulfil the third of the philosopher's requirements, would he or she ensure that any arborial adornment sent to me is a very small shrub or bush?

This book is certainly not a tree of knowledge. All that it attempts to do is to share the experiences of the writer, culled over four decades in the law, with others who have joined the ranks of the advocates more recently. Its only philosophy derives from the premise: 'It is a wise person who learns from his or her mistakes; a wiser who learns from the mistakes of others'. To some extent the book is a confessional.

Advocacy profoundly affects the lives of those who call upon the services of the advocate. A good, conscientious advocate can save an innocent person from being convicted—and it is difficult to imagine anything worse than being found guilty of an offence that one has not committed—or a guilty person from detention in an overcrowded, insanitary prison. It can provide comfort and consolation in the form of adequate damages for a person whose life has been ruined in a terrible road accident; it can ensure that a family stays on in their home in the face of a fraudulent claim by a greedy landlord—and a roof over one's head is almost as important as the provision of one's daily bread.

If this little book serves to impart something of the art of the advocate to those embarking on this important aspect of legal practice, and if it makes in some small measure for a happier relationship between the bench and those of both branches of the legal profession who have to argue the causes of their fellow citizens before the courts, the midnight oil burned on the writing and the typing of it will not have been in vain.

Eric Crowther
1984

1 Your first case

One thing of which you can be almost sure: you won't have much time to prepare your first case. If you plan to be a solicitor advocate the chances are that the client will come to see you the day before the hearing (possibly having quarrelled with all the other solicitors in the area first); if you are at the Bar, just out of pupillage, you will receive, at about 6.30 pm the night before, a brief bearing your name in place of that of a more eminent member of Chambers whose name has been scrubbed out by a diligent clerk, well-skilled in the art of deletion and substitution. The clerk will not have revealed the fact of its being your first case to your instructing solicitor. Do your best to ensure that he does not find out.

Two other things are almost as certain about your first case. You are unlikely ever to be paid for it—certainly if you are at the Bar. I did my first case about forty years ago. It was marked a guinea. I haven't received the fee yet. I did write to remind the solicitor concerned when I was made a magistrate in 1968 but he hasn't got around to paying me yet. It must be the recession. The other thing is that you will never forget your first case. You may do thousands of others—I hope you will—but you will never forget the first. The facts of my primary ordeal are still enshrined in my memory as clearly as if I had appeared in the case yesterday, and I will refer to some aspects of it later.

So, you won't have much time to prepare your first case, but you should have been preparing for it for months beforehand. This preparation should have taken various forms. First of all, you should have read of a number of books on the fringe of the law. There is only one real law book that I would advise a solicitor or a barrister to re-read after he has qualified, and that is *Cross on Evidence*. Evidence is the only legal subject that really matters when you are in court, because if you fail to object to the inadmissable question in time, the inadmissible answer is in, and English judges never utter the American piece of hypocrisy: 'I shall have that reply stricken from the record'. On the other hand if you object too often and unnecessarily you will get the reputation of being objectionable. So *Cross* is your legal Bible, a very present help when you are in trouble. I used to urge this on all my pupils when I was in practice at the Bar. I urged it so strongly that one of them took *Cross* on his honeymoon with him. He *is* still married, but he is no longer at the Bar. There's a lesson in this somewhere—something to do with keeping a sense of proportion in practice.

The other books, all very readable, that you should have digested before your first case are:

—*Learning the Law* by Professor Glanville Williams, to tell you a great deal about the profession on which you are just embarking.
—*The English Judge* by Henry Cecil (the late Judge H C Leon, MC), to tell you all about the judges before whom you will appear.
—*The English Magistracy* by Sir Frank Milton, former Chief Metropolitan Magistrate, to tell you all about the magistrates, lay and stipendiary, before whom you will appear.
—*Road Traffic Law* by Linda Dobbs and Mark Lucraft, because you are likely to be very involved in that in your early days.
—*The Sentence of the Court*, a Home Office publication, giving not only the maxima for all offences, but also some indication of sentencing policy as it has evolved; it is obtainable from Her Majesty's Stationery Office.
—*Principles of sentencing* by Professor D A Thomas.
—*The Modern Juvenile Court* by John Watson and Pat

Austin (my former Chief Clerk), to tell you about the drastic effect that the Children and Young Persons Act 1969 had on juvenile court proceedings. One possible result has been an immense increase in juvenile crime. More than half detected burglaries in England and Wales are committed by youngsters under seventeen. It follows that if you are going to 'do crime' you will spend a lot of time in your early days in the juvenile courts, and you had better know the procedure, which is quite different from that in adult magistrates' courts. You must also be well aware of the restrictions imposed by Parliament on custodial sentences for persons under twenty-one. These are to be found in s 1(4) and (4A) of the Criminal Justice Act 1988. There is an excellent article on this subject in the *Bulletin of the Judicial Studies Board*, No 3 of 1989.

—'The Code of Practice' accompanying the Police and Criminal Evidence Act 1984, which will indicate to you what to challenge in 'confessions', and when.

Mercifully, all these books are reasonably short and relatively inexpensive.

Now, before your first case appears, is the time to acquire your mastery over words—what 'Pendragon' in a brilliant article in the *Guardian Gazette* in May 1977 called 'Courtly English'—by wide general reading of the great works of British literature. Sir Walter Scott's lawyer Guy Mannering took a visitor into his Chambers and said: 'These are the tools of my trade', pointing to the great works of English (and no doubt especially Scottish) literature that abounded on his bookshelves. They are tools that you can always fall back on in times of crisis; they will come readily and naturally to your assistance in your closing addresses. So read them now, while you have time. Later on you will have a guilt complex if you read anything other than law reports. Your absorption of literary language—of 'Courtly English'—will prevent your slipping into the jargon of the social worker and declaring that your client has 'an on-going relationship with his siblings and his peers'. Some juveniles turn a sickly green when they hear these symptoms attributed to them, but they would be quite pleased to know that they got on well with their brothers and sisters and friends.

Do read some law reports, though, to get into the swing of things. It is useful to try to have regular access to the *Weekly Law Reports* or the *All England Reports.* To read the judgments of Lord Denning is to begin to believe that the law is really a simple thing, with the courts just trying to be fair; a view which only the Parliamentary draftsmen will be able to dispel.

So much for reading; what of speaking? Here, more than anywhere else, practice can make for perfection and it could be a tragedy if the first occasion on which you ever spoke in public were to be the occasion of your first case. So join a debating society—perhaps one unconnected with the law so that it won't matter if you make a fool of yourself—and make a point of getting up on your feet every time you go there; also join a public speaking class, if the local authority provides one in your district. Make sure you have some confidence in yourself before that first morning in court.

Lord Denning may have tried to be fair, but life itself is not always fair, and although you will have prepared your case far more carefully than your opponent, he may well be at an advantage because he 'knows the court' and you don't. Try to overcome this deficiency during your articles or pupillage by attending court with your principal or master whenever he has to make an appearance, and asking to go with someone else in the firm or Chambers if there is nothing more important for you to do. If you are in London, spend Saturdays if you can in the stipendiary magistrates' courts. Study the foibles of the judges and magistrates—they all have them, for the most part unconsciously. In the county courts there are 'landlords' judges' and 'tenants' judges', 'plaintiffs' judges' and 'defendants' judges', and in the magistrates' courts justices who are 'good over bail' and others who just follow the prosecution line; magistrates who appear anti-motorist, and others who will lean over back-wards to find 'exceptional hardship' when a lorry driver comes up for almost mandatory disqualification under the 'points system'. No amount of training or legislation will alter people's fundamental attitudes so as to produce robot-like consistency in penalties, and I for one should be sorry if it did, as ultimate consistency in penalties would also involve predictability in the consequences of committing offences, which would not be in the public interest. Another advantage of visiting the courts beforehand is that you can study the atmosphere and acoustics of the different courtrooms and decide how you will address them. The volume of voice needed to make yourself heard in the Lord Chief Justice's Court would sound like a supersonic boom in Court No 3 ('the Cocktail Bar') at Bow Street.

If, as luck will have it, you finish up, after all, in a court that you have never visited, get there early and tell other practitioners that it is your first case and ask 'What is the judge (or the beak) like here?'

Ours is, on the whole, a kindly profession and I have never known of anyone thinking that this was the occasion for a practical joke. You might also consider seeking the advice of the clerk to the court, especially if the matter is a highly technical one like licensing, about which few practitioners (or magistrates) know very much, but only do this if he comes into court early and does not seem unduly preoccupied.

'Won't I be nervous?' I can hear you asking. Of course you will. I hope you will always be a bit nervous, as otherwise you will appear over-confident and even arrogant and pompous, which are among the least attractive qualities to be found in young advocates. The good advocate is always nervous. I am sorry if that sounds discouraging, and I will qualify it by saying that as your experience grows, the period during which you will feel nervous upon rising to your feet will reduce from minutes to seconds. An Old Bailey judge who retired a few years ago and before whom I had frequently appeared when I was at the Bar—and he had usually terrified me when I was a young advocate—said this to me not long before his retirement: 'If I were starting at the Bar again, I wouldn't be so nervous of the judges. I'd realise that they would be nervous of me.' And I recognised, when I got to know him socially, that this brilliant judge who had at times appeared intellectually arrogant (he often gave the impression of knowing that he was quite the cleverest person in court) was in reality a very shy, modest, kindly man, selflessly dedicated to the ideals of justice.

One way of getting used to dealing with people and their problems is to give advice at a Legal Advice Centre (what used to be called in less—or possibly more—affluent times a Poor Man's Lawyer) or a Law Centre or Citizen's Advice Bureau. I attended two such centres weekly for many years: Cambridge House, in Camberwell, which provided me with my second brief before a very rude magistrate ('You and he didn't hit it off very well, did you dear?' asked my sympathetic Cockney lady client afterwards) and Toynbee Hall, where I had very distinguished predecessors in Lord Justice Birkett and Sir Frank Milton. When taking statements at these centres or offices try to do so without asking leading questions—an excellent training for the difficult art of examination-in-chief (of which more later). Young barristers in particular are recommended to attend Legal Advice Centres or Law Centres, for here is a rare opportunity for them to do a solicitor's work; they will probably grumble less about the way that solicitors prepare their briefs when they have had a little experience of trying to get a coherent statement from an inarticulate client.

So, the first case has arrived, and it's on tomorrow morning. No dinner with the loved one tonight. Let's hope they'll understand. If not, find someone else; or you may not get another case.

The first thing to do with your brief is to read it and prepare it. The secrets of success in advocacy, as in most aspects of life, are preparation and, I am afraid, hard work. This is what Paul Ysell wrote of Anatole France's preparation of *Jeanne d'Arc*:

> 'It had cost him twenty years' work. Every page had been corrected, remodelled, cut up with scissors. Such is the Master's method. On looking at his manuscripts, one is amazed to see what labour has been expended on that

apparent ease and unconstrained grace. It is a fine lesson for apprentices'.

Well, mercifully you will not have so long to prepare your first case; but do at least read your brief.

'Read your brief?' I can hear you exclaiming. 'What an extraordinary thing to say! Whoever would go into Court without having read his brief?' But they do.

A barrister appeared before me prosecuting in a case of ABH (actual bodily harm). (Don't use initials like: 'He got a CD for CD'.) He called his first witness, a medical witness. 'Are you Dr Singh Mbbs?' the barrister asked. 'No, no, I am Dr Singh. MBBS is my qualification', replied the doctor. Had that barrister read his brief?

If you want to be really good, prepare the case three times over. First; read it through thoroughly and make sure you understand it, underlining the matters that seem to need emphasis. Then go away and have a hot drink and come back and prepare it again, IMAGINING YOU HAVE BEEN BRIEFED BY THE OTHER SIDE. Some advocates seem surprised in court—even enraged—that there is another side. That is foolish intellectual arrogance. Don't let yourself be taken by surprise in that way.

And then another break, and return to deal with it again from your own side, preparing now to refute the arguments that you have raised in your role of devil's advocate.

Don't get confused by all this. Make sure that next morning you have it clear in your mind which side you are on!

Preparation involves looking up the relevant law, discovering what is the maximum sentence (counsel have sometimes been criticised in the Court of Appeal (Criminal Division) for allowing the inferior court to pass a sentence in excess of the maximum, an easy thing to do with the many changes brought about by recent legislation). Study the Criminal Law Act 1977 and the Criminal Justice Acts 1982 and 1988 and try to understand them—no mean task. If you are making a bail application familiarise yourself with all the exceptions to the right to bail set out in Pts I and II to Sched 1 to the 1976 Bail Act.

On the day of the hearing you will, I hope, remember to get dressed. Please dress soberly and discreetly, as a mark of respect for the court in which you will be a participant, and as a mark of respect for your client. If someone near and dear to me were taken ill, I would not have much confidence in the judgment of a doctor who turned up to treat his patient in a sweat shirt and jeans. And if I were at death's door and a doctor arrived in that condition I think it would have the effect of pushing me through. It does not matter how witnesses dress, but the advocate must dress properly.

Get up in good time, for you've got to be there early. Your fee as a barrister, whether the case is legally aided or privately paid, will include a notional sum for a conference at the door of the court. Even if you've had the chance of a conference beforehand in Chambers or your office (which is highly desirable and which you should always strive to arrange if at all possible, for your client will certainly welcome it) your lay client is entitled to have you there, half an hour in advance, to shake rather than hold his hand, to reassure him, to take any last minute instructions and to get on the right wavelength with him, you can also use this time to discuss the matter with the representative of the Crown Prosecution Service and, on a first appearance, to try to persuade him or her to let you have a glance at the prosecution witnesses' statements. There is no excuse, I repeat NO EXCUSE, for being late.

Getting to court early will enable you to get into the courtroom before the court sits. Make yourself comfortable, ensure that all your papers are in the correct order for you to conduct the case without shuffling or confusion. There will be a board on which, before the court sits, you should fill in your name, the name of the case and other details. Get attuned to the atmosphere of the court. Study the bench's reactions in other cases.

Wait for your case to be called on before you rise to your feet to open (always assuming that you are on the opening side).

If, despite your valiant efforts in this your first case your client is convicted, or if he pleaded guilty from the outset, you will be required to make a plea in mitigation. This is a subtle, gentle, neglected and vitally important art, which I study in depth later in this book.

It will be noted that everything that I have said about your first case has been based on the assumption that it takes place in a magistrates' court. It might equally well be in the county court. (If you are a young barrister it might be in the Court of Appeal: I hope for your sake, not. I have seen disaster lie that way.) My own first case was in the Bloomsbury County Court, presided over by the senior county court judge, His Honour Judge Alun Pugh QC. It was a judgment summons. I didn't know what a judgment summons was until I got that brief, but next morning when I arrived at the court, having spent the night with the Green Book (*County Court Practice*) I was the greatest living authority on judgment summonses. The brief made it clear that there were only two things the solicitor wanted:

(i) a suspended committal order against the recalcitrant debtor, and
(ii) an order for costs with *certificate for counsel.*

These words were underlined, and it was emphasised that if I failed to get such a certificate there would be no money with which to pay my guinea. (I did get it, but as I have said, I haven't been paid yet. But then, Dickens said that solicitors were sometimes slow in doing things).

As I changed in the crowded robing-room, due to my nervousness I broke my collar-stud. Just as I was uttering some 'un-Courtly English' I observed to my great horror my sister coming up the path of the court. At first I thought that she must be a defendant in some matter that she had kept secret from the family, but then I realised that foolishly I had revealed the previous evening over dinner (which I had been unable to eat) that I had my first brief next day, and, even more foolishly, had answered (truthfully) questions concerning time and venue. Anyway, I was able to send her off in search of a new collar-stud and because I (and she) had followed my advice to set off early (but separately) in case of disaster I had it *in situ* in time for the sitting of the court.

The defendant was a rascally ex-Colonel who, despite many promises, had not paid a small debt (under £30, but this was in 1952) to my lay client, a virtuous ex-Squadron leader. (The had been comrades in arms during the Second World War.) Once I started cross-examining the Colonel, I forgot about my sister at the back of the court and got rather carried away with my own enthusiasm. The extremely kindly judge realised that it was my first case—I am able to say this because he afterwards became a good personal friend—and so he permitted me to go on much longer than is customary in such small matters, but he did intervene when I demanded of the defendant. 'Do you not agree with me that you are despicable?'

'Well, Mr Crowther,' he remarked, smilingly, 'that sounds a little harsh', and, turning to the defendant, he asked 'Do you agree with learned counsel that you are despicable?'

'No, Your Honour', replied the Colonel (to my great surprise). 'I do not. I'm only a poor, old, honest man.'

'And what do you have to say to that, Mr Crowther?' the judge asked, beaming, for he was really enjoying the situation.

'Well, Your Honour', I replied, 'he doesn't look poor, and he doesn't look old, and I don't think he's honest.'

The smile vanished from the judge's face. He looked at me severely. 'You must never express your own opinion in court', he said seriously. 'Your opinion of the witness, or of the case, is quite irrelevant. What you should have said was: "And I leave it to your Honour to decide if he is honest". Never again let me hear you say "I think" or "in my opinion" in this court.'

So I left the court, victorious but ashamed, having learned three lessons that morning, in addition to the necessity to arrive early:

(1) do not tell your family or your friends of your first case. They will come, and disaster will befall you;
(2) do take a spare collar-stud if you are going to a court where you must robe; and

(3) most important of all: never express your opinion, or views, or thoughts in court. I never did so again in the next sixteen and a half years (but I sometimes did thereafter!)

2 Integrity and preparation in advocacy

In the previous chapter I referred to the lessons that I learned from the first case in which I ever appeared in court. I dwelt on my own experience on the basis of the maxim that 'It is a wise man who learns from his mistakes but a wiser one who learns from the mistakes of others'. I should now like to refer to two other 'firsts' of mine: my first appearance in the Court of Criminal Appeal, now the Court of Appeal (Criminal Division), and my first appearance in the Civil Division of the Court of Appeal. On each occasion the court was presided over by one of the great judges of our age, before whom I was appearing for the first time: Lord Goddard and Lord Denning respectively. I had been called about two years when I had to appear before the formidable 'Lord God'—as I am afraid he was rather blasphemously called by the Bar of those days. The matter arose in the following way.

I was briefed to appear at the City of London Quarter Sessions to defend a lad of seventeen who had pleaded guilty before the Alderman at the Mansion House to being in possession of an offensive weapon, a sock filled with sand. The defendant had one previous conviction, for stealing a glove by finding when he was nine, and the Alderman, in view of his 'character and antecedents' had committed him in custody to the Quarter Sessions for sentence, with a view to Borstal training. The boy lived with and supported his widowed mother, was in work and his employer spoke well of him. He lived in a big block of council flats in the East End of London, and the caretaker of the whole estate and several neighbours were prepared to come to court to say what a kind and helpful boy he was, especially in running errands for old people, lighting their fires, etc.

Unfortunately, in those early days at the Bar I did not know where the City of London Quarter Sessions were held, and my then Clerk, who was more used to civil work, assured me that the solicitors had a mistake and really intended the County of London Sessions, which in the post-war days were held in what had formerly been Marylebone Swimming Baths, to which I repaired. The case was not listed in any of the four courts sitting there, and I returned, worried and puzzled, to Chambers, only to learn that the City of London Quarter Sessions in fact sat four times a year at the Old Bailey, that my client had appeared there that morning, had said nothing and had not called any of the witnesses who were there to speak on his behalf (he having expected me to rise from among the serried ranks of the bewigged before him to conduct his defence) and had been sent to Borstal by the then Recorder of London, Sir Gerald Dodson.

By the time the news reached me the court had risen, and I regarded the Recorder as *functus officio*, so I set off for Wormwood Scrubs Prison where I found my client, very forlorn and depressed in the wing set aside for boys awaiting allocation to Borstal institutions. I told him what had happened, advised that his only possible remedy now lay in appeal to the Court of Criminal Appeal, obtained the requisite forms from the prison staff and set about helping him to draft the first notice of appeal that I had ever seen. Under 'Grounds of Appeal', I wrote: 'My counsel went to the wrong court and in consequence no mitigation was advanced on my behalf and none of the character witnesses who attended court to speak for me was called', and I got him to sign it. Weeks passed before the case was listed to come on before a court presided over by the Lord Chief Justice, with Hilbery J and Hallett J as the other members. My friends at the Bar advised me that this was not the ideal tribunal for my purpose, as any practitioner who remembers those two other quite frightening 'old school' judges will readily agree. I saw two convicted murderers' appeals disposed of somewhat, as it seemed to me, summarily, and the dejected appellants led away towards their deaths. I wondered what was going to happen to me. In my mind's eye I could already see the evening paper's banner headline: 'Barrister went to wrong court. Disgraceful says LCJ' and, next morning: 'Barrister Disbarred'. At about ten past four my case, the thirty-seventh in a list of forty, was called on, and I rose weakly to my feet for the first time in that enormous courtroom: 'May it please your Lordships, I appear—'. 'Wait a minute', said Goddard gruffly, 'we haven't read your notice of appeal yet. You want us to read that, I suppose?' 'I'm not sure', I murmured. He studied it, and so did the other two, and he conferred briefly with his brethren, talking with his hand in front of his mouth. 'Mr Crowther', he said eventually. 'My Lord', I replied, waiting for the worst. 'You don't want to say too much about this case, I should imagine.' 'Not if it can be helped, my Lord.' 'I didn't think you would. This young man's been punished far too much already. He'll be put on probation for two years.'

This is my answer to those who say, as Bernard Levin did in an article published in *The Times* a day or two after the former Lord Chief Justice's death—note the timing—that Lord Goddard enjoyed being unkind to young barristers. He had a wonderful opportunity so to be if he had wished, but instead he did everything he could to save me from embarrassment for my mistake. Moreover, the offence was one of a kind that he was supposed to detest—potential violence by a youngster. Yet he could set all that aside because he felt that this particular young man had been unjustly treated.

In the previous chapter I endeavoured to imply that preparation must be so intensive that you must be prepared for everything—even the totally unexpected; and I said that I hoped that no barrister would find himself forced into the higher courts too early. In this I had in mind the sad experience of a barrister whom I will call Mr Young. This was not his name, but the epithet fitted him. The case found its way into the law report of *The Times* under the surprisingly sensational title: 'Parents Beware!'

It was an appeal from a judgment of Judge Southall

sitting in the Saxmundham County Court and it was all about school fees. My opponent there, and in the Court of Appeal, was a distinguished junior who is now a High Court Judge. I will call him 'Mr Progress', as he has done so well.

The case was listed second on a Wednesday. We all turned up but it soon became apparent that the case in front of ours was going to last a very long time, and Mr Progress took a calculated risk by starting on an accident case in another part of the Royal Courts of Justice, leaving his pupil, Mr Young, to hold the fort. I remained in Lord Denning's court, not so much because I was more virtuous than my opponent, as because I had no other work at that time. Mr Young and I sat throughout Wednesday, throughout Thursday and throughout most of Friday. These were the days in which 'judicial time' was regarded as one of the most precious commodities in the courts. Then at about three o'clock on the Friday afternoon it happened. Counsel for the appellant in the preceding case, who had been on his feet for over two and a half days, completed his submissions and sat down, and Lord Denning called over the other two judges and they got into a huddle and then Lord Denning said: 'We don't need to hear the Respondent in this matter. The appeal is dismissed with costs. Call the next case please', and the Associate did so.

Mr Young bestirred himself and asked me 'What do I do?' 'Get Progress', I said 'I'll keep them at bay until he comes'. A few minutes later Mr Young came scurrying back. 'He's cross-examining the defendant', he said, 'I pulled his gown and he uttered a very rude remark.'

By now Lord Denning was getting restless. I had told him, during Mr Young's absence, that I was for the Respondent and that Mr Progress was in another court but was expected along shortly. 'Well, who's that young man?' asked Lord Denning. 'I'm Mr Progress's pupil', Young managed to murmur. 'Good, good', said Lord Denning encouragingly. 'Open the case, please'. 'Oh, no', exclaimed Mr Young in horror. 'Well, you've read it, haven't you?' asked the presiding judge. 'Er, no', admitted Mr

Young. 'Oh dear, oh dear', said Lord Denning sadly. 'What have you been doing these last two days? Some young men would give their ears for a chance like this. You're not going to throw it away, are you?' 'Yes please, my Lord' said Mr Young.

'Well' sighed Lord Denning, 'it's all a great pity, but we can't lose time'. (Lord Denning was unfailingly courteous, yet permitted no waste of time in his court. It was marvellous to see him handle the really eccentric litigant in person, who would go away, usually having lost his case, but feeling that justice had been done, although Lord Denning had taken the minimum time compatible with fairness to bring matters to a proper conclusion.) 'You'd better open the case, Mr Crowther'.

'But my Lord, I'm on the other side', I protested.

'I know, but you're a very fairminded man, I'm sure.' (How he was sure I shall never know, as it was my first appearance before our greatest judge, and I have never thought fit to ask him.) 'So please open the case.'

I did, for about three-quarters of an hour, as neutrally and dispassionately as I could, determining to save my histrionics for my closing address. Towards four o'clock I said, 'My Lords, I don't feel I can continue further, as now I have reached the contentious part of the case, and Mr Progress would be better qualified to handle his argument than I'.

'Very well', said Lord Denning, 'we've only wasted a quarter of an hour. Let's hope that Mr Progress will be back with us on Monday, or' (looking meaningfully at the unhappy Young) 'someone who can carry on the appellant's case.'

On the next Monday Mr Progress miraculously appeared, profuse with apologies—I don't know if his accident case had been settled and, if so, on what terms—and the case was able to procede in a more conventional manner.

The lesson I learned that day was that one must be prepared for anything—even to conduct the case of the other side; and thereafter I always prepared all my cases from the point of view of both sides, which in any event makes one far better able to meet the arguments of the other side, when they arise.

Young solicitors may feel that, unless and until some of the provisions of the Courts and Legal Services Bill become law, the two cases I have just cited are not of much interest to them, but I do assure you that the principles to be derived from them—absolute honesty and integrity within the court, and the most diligent preparation of your case from the point of view of both sides—are equally applicable to every type of court. An American lawyer who came around with me for two weeks many years ago by arrangement with the American Bar Association started off by asking me: 'Say, are your judges soft in the head or something? They seem to believe what the lawyers are telling them!' but he finished up by describing the English legal profession as 'a priesthood'. This is in keeping with former Vice-Chancellor Megarry's observation: 'I would as soon trust the word of a barrister as that of a bishop!'

This is as it should be. It makes for a much happier atmosphere in court and a far better relationship between Bench and Bar if the judge or the magistrates feel that they can rely on the solicitor or barrister appearing before them; and it saves a lot of time if they can accept facts recited to them without having to check up on everything. And the client who feels that his advocate has so mastered the facts of his case that he is (albeit only temporarily) living his life for him is a very relieved and contented client. That is what the lawyer is there for: to take some of the strain off his client so that he will feel at ease as a witness.

The Bar is fortunate in being a very small profession. The Temple is the smallest village in England. If a barrister has a disagreement with a judge or a stipendiary magistrate in the morning it will be all over the Inns by tea-time. Barristers are not by nature more virtuous than solicitors. The fact that there appear, proportionately, to be fewer 'black sheep' among them is due in large measure to this village atmosphere. This is a factor surely worthy of consideration on the question of extension of rights of audience.

As a very young barrister I went to a county court to

defend a possession action. The case in front of mine was settled and at 10.35 we were ready to go on. One of the counsel in the earlier case, someone I did not know at all, took me on one side. 'Do you know your opponent?' he asked. 'No', I replied. 'Well, watch him. That's all I want to say. Watch him,' he adjured.

It was good advice. Every unfair point that could be taken was taken. Each time he played the game unfairly I sought to show him up. At the end of a long and acrimonious day the judge began his judgment as follows: 'Usually in heavily contested cases of this kind one is grateful to both advocates for their assistance. In this case I am grateful to only one advocate. I am grateful to Mr Crowther for exposing all the scandalous efforts of his opponent to deceive and mislead this court, a matter that I shall have to consider taking further.' But I would not, with my inexperience then, have thought of challenging my opponent so much, but for those cautionary words whispered to me by a complete stranger in the robing room. A good reputation among one's colleagues is worth a lot.

More recently, when I was sitting as a recorder with a jury at the Crown Court, the same barrister, now quite elderly, appeared before me. He never achieved judicial office; but he was, I regret to say, as wily and untrustworthy as ever. If I may be forgiven a mixed metaphor: 'The black sheep had not changed his spots!'

3 Advocacy before magistrates—lay and stipendiary

In the first chapter I envisaged you having your first case in a magistrates' court. But there are, of course, two kinds of magistrates, lay and stipendiary, and the techniques of advocacy before them are very different. There are about 28,000 lay justices in England and Wales, sitting occasionally, and usually in Benches of three (as they decide cases by a majority). These justices of the peace are not lawyers, they give their services voluntarily and are known as 'The Great Unpaid'. The stipendiary magistrates, of whom there are now about sixty-five (more than fifty sitting in London) sitting alone in criminal matters are qualified solicitors or barristers drawn from private practice or the public service and are paid. The epithet 'Great' is usually omitted when referring to them, perhaps because they are not paid greatly! Between 1829 and 1962 there were no lay justices in Inner London except for juvenile and licensing matters, but Lord Gardiner, when Lord Chancellor, reintroduced the lays to London, and now your chances of getting a lay bench are almost equal to your chances of appearing before a stipendiary; probably greater if the case is contested.

If the case is contested, try to find out whether the Bench before which you will appear is going to be lay or stipendiary, because it will certainly affect your preparation of the case. But be prepared to be flexible: your case may be switched from one court to another.

In court, before a stipendiary, if you are prosecuting,

open with the words: 'May it please you sir (or madam), I appear for the Crown Prosecution Service and the defendant is represented by my (learned) friend Mr Wimpish'. (In a subtle form of defamation, barristers usually omit the word 'learned' when introducing a solicitor opponent.) This is the term of address always used by barristers. For reasons that are a mystery to me but perhaps derive from from the bad old days when mayors were *ex officio* justices of the peace, solicitors usually address the Bench, lay or stipendiary, male or female, as 'Your Worship'. This is quite acceptable provided that it is not allowed to degenerate into 'Your Wash-up'. (Defendants in person have on occasions addressed me as 'Your Majesty', 'Your Grace' and 'Your Worshipful Highness' on the principle, as one Irish defendant observed to me, that 'politeness costs nothing and the future is uncertain', but these examples should not be emulated, as flattery will get you nowhere. They are, however, couched in 'Courtly English'.) As an alternative to 'Your Worships' for a plural lay Bench (or a stipendiary sitting with lay justices, as frequently happens in the matrimonial and juvenile courts) try to identify the sex of the chairman and then use the format 'May it please you, sir (or madam), and members of the Bench' (I will discuss forms of address in other courts in a later chapter). There is a temptation to address observations and argument to the chairman only and this is a great mistake. All the justices have an equal say and an equal vote, so embrace them all (not literally, of course, but with your eyes). Even in the Crown Court, where lay justices sit with the Crown Court judges on appeals and committals for sentence, they are in effect judges because if there are two of them they can outvote the professional judge (and occasionally do).

Lord Parker was a Lord Chief Justice of brilliant intellect who would grasp the point early in a case and soon make up his mind. He was never discourteous: he just appeared to 'switch off' at an early stage in the proceedings. The signal was when he cupped his chin in his hands. I found this somewhat disconcerting, especially as I was usually for appellants who did not seem to him to have much merit in their cases. So when he did 'switch off' metaphorically (unlike an elderly county court judge who literally switched off his immense hearing box when he had had enough!) I used to transfer my attention and argument to the other two members of the Bench. After a while Lord Parker would appear upset by this and would seek to re-enter the arena by asking questions; his interest had been recaptured. (Not that it ever did my clients much good. His was not my luckiest court.) But if you feel that you have established a rapport with a member of the Bench (or of the jury in the Crown Court) concentrate on him or her and do not let that person lose your attention. If they are on your side now they may stay with you in the retiring room.

After the dramatis personæ have been introduced, in the manner already indicated, you have to decide, if you are prosecuting, whether to make an opening speech or not. In general, before a stipendiary, don't make an opening speech unless the case is one of exceptional complexity or difficulty. If you do open he will immediately think that it is a case of difficulty—difficulty for you; in other words that you have a weak case from the start.

But there are exceptions to this general rule. A Nigerian barrister prosecuted before me in a company fraud case. He opened it at some length. He was right to do so. He had correctly guessed that I knew nothing about company law and needed to be 'reminded', as he tactfully put it. Even as a student I went to the lectures more for the company than for the law.

With a lay Bench it is often wise to open the case, to let the justices know what the case is about from the outset, to try to get them thinking your way as early as possible, and to explain the relevant law to them. This is one of the three occasions on which you will have an opportunity to present your case: once in opening, once through the mouths of your witnesses in examination-in-chief and finally in cross examination of the defendant or respondent. Remember that you are not allowed a closing address as prosecutor in a magistrates' court, unless the defence has raised a point of law (and then your reply must be restricted to arguing the law).

Never open too high. If your witnesses let you down the Bench will lose faith both in you and your case. 'Moderation in all things' is a good maxim of advocacy.

The late Clifford Reston became in 1966, again under the aegis of Lord Gardiner, the Lord Chancellor's first Training Officer for justices of the peace in Inner London. Before that, such qualities as 'good common sense' and 'gut reactions' were deemed to be enough. They were not. The quality of lay justice has improved immensely as a result of the work of Mr Reston and his successors, the most recent of whom is John Greenhill, with whom I am very pleased, as Chairman of the Inner London Training Sub-Committee, to have worked in close harness. This was a great responsibility for both of us.

Mr Reston once estimated to me that cases take three times as long before lay justices as they do before stipendiaries, and the greater celerity of the professional is borne out by Sir Thomas Skyrme in his admirable book, *The Changing Image of the Magistracy* in which he estimates that forty-two lay justices would have to be appointed to dispose of the work done by one metropolitan magistrate. Those who argue that the merit of lay justice is that it is cheap because the justices give their services free, are wrong. It is more expensive. Clerks in court are paid, ushers are paid, gaolers are paid, advocates are paid (sometimes) and heating and lighting bills pile up, all costing therefore three times as much. If the main advantage of the lay justice system were its cheapness, I should be against it. I hate the idea of justice on the cheap. But it is not its main advantage. Its main merit is far more important. It lies in the involvement of the ordinary citizen in the administration of justice, removing from law some of its 'Ivory Tower' image; it is justice by the people for the people. And the quality, in London at any rate (I am not qualified to speak of the provinces and the countryside), of lay justice has improved immeasurably since training justices became compulsory in 1966.

From his experience as a Senior Chief Clerk Mr Reston

told me that advocates argue their cases at three times the length before lay justices that they employ before the 'stipes'. He did not complain of this. He felt that they were justified in so doing, in treating the lay justices, sitting perhaps once a fortnight, as they would treat a jury. They are a superior kind of jury because they have had some training in the evaluation of evidence and have—most of them—learned to set aside their personal prejudices when sitting on the Bench.

'If I say a thing three times it must be true' remarked one of the characters in Lewis Carroll's *The Hunting of the Snark*, whilst more poetically Robert Browning advocated:

> 'Be like the wise thrush; he sings each song twice over
> Lest you should think he never could recapture
> That first fine careless rapture.'

But birds are not popular in magistrates' courts. I am referring to parrots, when they start repeating themselves.

Even so, greater length, greater involvement in detail is permissible with lay justices, just as it is necessary with juries, and for much the same reason. The first essential quality in any good advocate is the ability to see the point of a case. All professional judges have risen from the ranks of the legal profession, and most, one hopes, were good lawyers and good advocates. They ought therefore to be able to grasp the essential points of a case more rapidly than people from almost any other calling in life.

Judges ought to be thoroughly familiar with the onus and burden of proof—though not all have consistently manifested this quality in the past—and with the basic requirements of the more familiar Acts of Parliament like the Theft Act 1968, the Bail Act 1976, the Police and Criminal Evidence Act 1984 (ss 76 and 78 of which are particularly germane when the advocate in a criminal case is challenging the admissibility of a confession) and the Criminal Justice Act 1988. They have been known to sigh rather noticeably when an advocate has reached his peroration about 'the golden thread running through the English criminal law that the case against the accused has to be proved beyond all reasonable doubt' (instead of simply asking: 'Can you really be sure in this case?') An advocate who on a bail application told me: 'I shall now address you on the statutory requirements affecting the grant and refusal of bail', looked rather hurt when I said 'You will not'. 'Why not?' he enquired. 'Because after dealing with them almost daily for many years I have acquired a working knowledge of them', I replied, and I am glad to say that he was wise enough not to pursue the matter any further.

My wife is a lay justice. On her sitting days she tends to discuss her cases in the evenings. It is a sort of busman's holiday for me, but you should not be a lawyer unless you always enjoy the law. A few years ago she recited all the facts of a contested motoring case and asked me 'What would you have done?' I said that I would have acquitted, and gave my reason. 'Well', said my wife, 'we all felt that, but the solicitor never mentioned that point so we thought there couldn't be anything in it and we convicted. I've been feeling unhappy about it ever since.' Whether the solicitor did not mention the point that would have assured an acquittal because he did not see it, or because he thought that it was too obvious to mention, we shall never know, but there is no doubt that the defendant was worse off because he had paid for a solicitor than he would have been had he defended himself. Never let that be said of your advocacy! In fact the point need not have been made before a stipendiary, and all the justices in this case were aware of it and would have acted upon it, if only the solicitor had mentioned it. This affords a clear example of what I mean when I say that the technique of advocacy is different before lay magistrates and 'stipes'.

Another difference lies in the role of the clerk. In days gone by some clerks ruled their lay Benches with rods of iron. In 1952 I saw a clerk send a man to prison for six weeks for maintenance arrears without any consultation with the three lay justices who were supposed to be adjudicating and without their uttering a word. (I am bound to admit that I did not utter a word of protest either. I was very newly called and sensed that something was wrong, but wondered if I had any *locus standi* in a case in which

I was not instructed; I did not then know the expression *amicus curiæ*, although I doubt if this particular clerk would have regarded me as an 'amicus' if I had intervened.) Lord Goddard put a stop to a lot of this sort of nonsense by ruling that clerks should not retire with their justices except when specifically invited to do so to advise them on a point of law. That did not prevent a clerk at Barnet advising the justices in open court in what I regarded as a particularly weak case from the prosecution's standpoint that there was 'plenty of evidence on which they could convict', or a clerk at Reading in 1968 telling me not to apply for bail because 'I never allow my justices to grant bail in robbery cases'. (He got his way with the justices—if not with me—but at the defendant's trial, after the defendant had spent three and a half months in custody, the late and much lamented Sebag Shaw J stopped the case and awarded him £750 costs. He was, I believe—and the judge believed—an innocent man; it was a pure identity case which, after *R* v *Turnbull,* would never have been committed.) Abuses of authority like this by clerks are nowadays rare—I had nothing but helpfulness and kindness from most of my clerks in London for over twenty years, and I believe that most advocates would say the same—but they have to be guarded against and prevented by the advocate.

But the clerk has a positive duty to prevent the court from making a mistake in law. One hopes that such intervention is rarely necessary in stipendiary courts, but I will confess that there have been occasions on which I have been grateful to my clerks for saving me, forensically, from a fate worse than death. If there is law in your case, and the court comprises a lay bench, the chances are that the magistrates will invite the clerk to advise them on the law when they retire. (They would be unwise not to do so.) It follows that you should try to involve the clerk in the legal argument, by mentioning him or her as their ultimate adviser in case of doubt, and by looking at him or her from time to time during your presentation of the case, just as you will seek to engage the attention of the 'book-ends' (as the justices not in the chair are frequently disrespectfully called—by the justices themselves). If, but only if, you are sure that the law is on your side, you can say: 'As your learned clerk will doubtless advise you when you retire . . .' but be quite certain of your ground before adopting this tactic; it could have disastrous consequences if the clerk were to go the other way. As most magistrates' courts libraries are not very well endowed, it will be helpful and appreciated if you can take along sufficient photostat copies of the reports you intend to refer to. Expect the clerk to intervene more in the lay justices' court, but do not put up with harassment by the clerk, if it is putting you off your stroke. If this occurs (and happily it is a very rare phenomenon nowadays) appeal politely to the chairman. You will usually find that he or she will say: 'I think it might be better if our learned clerk did not intervene any more'

I mentioned relevancy a moment ago. Even though I encouraged you to take a little longer, to be a little more leisurely in your approach to the lay bench, nothing that is not relevant to the case in hand should find its way into your questioning or your argument. In my role of Chairman of the Inner London Justices' Training Sub-Committee I found that justices often complained bitterly about the long-windedness and seemingly endless repetition of some advocates. I advised them, when they were really fed up, to ask this question: 'To what issue in this case is that line of questioning directed?'

It is the most devastating question you can be asked, and, if you are doing your job properly, you should always be in a position to answer it satisfactorily. Don't just murmur: 'It goes to credit' or you may meet with the rejoinder from the magistrate: 'Then you're bound by the answer, and you've had the answer, so move on to something else'.

In my view lay justices do not intervene enough in cases of unwarranted prolixity of advocates. Because they have been taught to keep quiet during the hearing, you seldom have any indication what they are thinking until they announce their verdict for which, regrettably as I think (though many disagree with me), they rarely give their reasons anyway. The fact that you have no indication of the way the wind is blowing is another reason for having to explore every avenue.

The stipendiary is more predictable, because he does join in with the occasional question or barbed aside, but he is often a more difficult, more prickly, and in some cases less courteous tribunal. The stipendiary, usually sitting in Court No 1, has to deal with the applications and his remands and the overnight charges and probably a hundred minor motoring matters. He is the victim of the 'Tyranny of the Daily List'. He's got to get through it, and he's not going to let you prevent him from doing so by inordinately lengthy flights of oratory. You will have to concentrate all your power, briefly, on the main issues in the case. The ABC of successful magistrates' court advocacy is to be alert, brisk and courteous. For this reason the stipendiary courts are the best places for new advocates to cut their teeth and to learn to be good advocates, receptive of a hint when it comes from the Bench ('I'm minded to follow the suggestion in the Social Enquiry Report' is usually a clear signal to sit down), capable of seeing and stressing the main point in the case, and utterly familiar with the vital rules of evidence.

4 The plea in mitigation: a gentle art

In the early stages of an advocate's career he envisages a future of superintendents of police crumbling in the witness box as a result of his devastating cross-examination, and murmuring just before collapsing into the arms of the court matron conveniently standing just behind: 'Don't ask me any more, sir. I admit that I tortured your client to write out his confession and that my testimony has been a tissue of lies from beginning to end, and I verballed your client from the moment I said "Good morning, Mr Sykes" to him.' In real life it doesn't happen like that. I only once in seventeen years managed to persuade a police officer that he might be wrong, and he was a temporary detective constable who immediately afterwards resumed uniform duty.

In real life, in England and Wales, approximately 92 per cent of those charged with criminal offences plead Guilty. (These figures vary, of course, from year to year, but remain reasonably constant, if still only approximate.) Of those who plead Not Guilty, approximately 97 per cent are tried by magistrates and only 3 per cent by juries.

Of the 97 per cent tried by magistrates a little over 60 per cent are found guilty. Of the 3 per cent tried by juries about half are convicted (a slightly lower proportion in London).

Each defendant who pleads or is found guilty is entitled to make or have made on his behalf a plea in mitigation.

It follows that a plea in mitigation is called for in at least nineteen out of twenty criminal cases. It can make all the difference between prison and a non-custodial sentence, and to many people, liberty is almost as important as life itself. To a lorry driver, due for disqualification under the points system, the eloquent advancement of 'exceptional mitigating circumstances' can save a man from losing the only source of livelihood open to him at a time of high unemployment.

In Henry Cecil's delightful book *Brothers-in-Law,* when Roger Thursby's pupil-master Grimes heard that Thursby had his first plea to do at the Old Bailey he simply advised him: 'Tell 'em the tale, my boy, tell 'em the tale'.

That is not good enough (although it appears to be good enough for some advocates). The plea in mitigation is a gentle art, a sophisticated art, a vital art and, alas, a sadly neglected art.

How long should the plea last? It is a difficult question to answer, as the amount of material available varies so much. Assuming one defendant and one charge, I would recommend five minutes in a magistrates' court, eight to ten at the Crown Court, as the cases there are normally more serious. But I have heard an eminent silk mitigate for one hour, and every minute of it seemed well spent. On the other hand I heard Mr Seaton, formerly Chairman of Inner London Sessions, ask counsel who had been on his feet only a short time: 'When it is so obvious that nothing at all can be said in this man's favour, why don't you just gracefully admit it and sit down?'

This struck me as being rather unfair. Surely nobody is so bad that 'nothing at all can be said in his favour'? You have to think of your client, sitting anxiously behind you, hanging on your every word. But it is true that sometimes the best result can be achieved by saying very little

In the mid-1960s I was briefed on behalf of a man who was going to plead guilty to a number of charges of incest with his two little daughters. The case was listed at the Old Bailey on a Friday afternoon. I saw the defendant for the first time in the cells that lunch time.

'Who's the judge?' he asked anxiously.

'Mr Justice Melford Stevenson', I replied.

'Oh Christ!' he exclaimed.

'Why do you say that?' I enquired innocently.

'Well, I've been told that I'll get five years for this from any judge except Melford, but with him I'll get eight.'

It was true that incest was not one of Melford's favourite offences.

'Well what would you like me to say on your behalf?' I asked, changing the subject slightly.

'There's nothing you can say, is there, for someone who's done what I've done', he replied morbidly.

I decided that it would be politic to withdraw at this point, and did so.

The case in front of mine was one of a City of London policeman, with many awards and commendations for bravery, who had broken into two shops on his 'beat' at night and stolen goods to the value of less than £100. His counsel mitigated for over an hour. Although the judge did not interrupt, it was plain from his expression that he was not finding the mitigation a pleasing experience, but the advocate was thick-skinned as well as long-winded. (He is now a Member of Parliament.) There were few people in Court No 1 of the Bailey that Friday afternoon, and the judge contented himself with indicating his boredom by looking at the clock and occasionally making facial grimaces at me. I began to feel that things were looking brighter for my client, though not for the unhappy policeman. When the torrent of mitigation had finally dried up, the judge said simply 'Four years' and the former policeman, now a prisoner, was led away.

My defendant was now brought up. He pleaded guilty to all the charges and the distasteful facts were recited in some detail. I was then invited to mitigate. 'My Lord', I said, 'I am specifically instructed by the defendant that there is no mitigation in this case but perhaps, when one thinks about it, that is the strongest possible mitigation.' He got two years, I achieved this with only thirty words, and always regarded it as one of my greatest triumphs on a plea.

There is a Queen's Counsel of my old Chambers, who can usually be relied on for a very thorough, moving and lengthy plea. Yet many years ago before me at Bow Street he achieved an excellent result with a minimum of words by seizing on the salient, indisputable point of the case. An Australian was charged with theft of an enormous quantity of clothing 'on or before' a certain date. His hotel room had been raided and all these garments had been found tucked away in cupboards. He refused to say anything at all to the police as to how or when he had acquired them, and they did not know, but he did plead guilty before me. Australian shoplifters were not very popular at that time. They were chartering planes to come to London and paying the charter fees out of the proceeds of their raids on our shops. Some courts had imposed heavy custodial sentences on some of them. Counsel addressed me in these terms: 'Sir, you will see that three months ago this defendant was given twelve months imprisonment suspended for two years at the Crown Court for similar offences. I represented him there, and even more property was involved on that occasion than on this. He instructs me that he stole the property involved in this charge before he appeared at the Crown Court. There is absolutely no evidence at all to refute that contention. In my submission it would be most unjust if he were to lose his liberty today just because he did not have the courage to own up to this lot when the Crown Court judge gave him such a marvellous chance three months ago.'

There was nothing in this plea to appeal to the emotions, but it was clearly logically and legally right. I decided to fine the defendant the maximum (£400 in those days) with no time to pay (which one could do in those days—indeed one still can if the defendant is unlikely to remain for long in the United Kingdom) and I was a little disconcerted to observe the speed and skill with which the defendant peeled off to the gaoler a sufficient number of 'tenners' from an enormous bunch of notes contained in his hip pocket.

It's a serious business, the plea in mitigation, requiring careful preparation and attention to tactics. Tactics worked in both the cases just recited. And 'knowing your judge' and getting used to the atmosphere of the court helped in my own case, too. Sir Samuel Romilly wrote: 'Often the very same circumstance is considered by one judge as a matter of extenuation, but by another as high aggravation of the crime'.

Drink is an example of this. One of Mr Seaton's predecessors as Chairman of the Inner London Sessions was Archie Cockburn QC. He did not regard drink as an excuse for crime, rather as an additional manifestation of greed. 'He took it quite voluntarily, nobody forced it down his throat', I heard him say many times. And I think he was right. I myself have often said, when drunkenness has been put forward as an excuse for a serious assault such as a glassing in a public house: 'I would much rather be assaulted by a sober man than by a drunken man, you can reason with a sober man, but you can't reason with a drunken man.' And if all the public houses and off-licences in London were to be closed down, the London stipendiaries would be in severe danger of joining the ranks of the unemployed. So, 'Know your court!'.

'All the other workers were doing it' I have heard advanced in mitigation in cases of thefts by employees. But some judges have observed that if this is the case there is need for a deterrent sentence and have passed one. This sort of thing is better left unsaid. There is a good deal of selection and rejection involved in the good plea in mitigation. Don't give the court a lecture on criminology. I was very impressed when I was informed once by young counsel that 'the Lambrosian theory of punishment has been superseded since the publication of Baer's *Der Verbrecher in Anthropologischen Beziehung*, but it did not help me much with the problem of how to deal with his client who had just pleaded guilty to attempted theft.

Even so, the plea in mitigation is a serious business. Never appear to be enjoying yourself at the defendant's expense, for he is in peril. There are I think plenty of occasions for humour in court (although that great advocate Sir Norman Birkett QC advised: 'Never introduce humour'). But the plea in mitigation is certainly not one of them. When you are instructed on behalf of the prosecution, don't, in the rather unattractive criminal terminology, 'put the boot in'. Remember when in that situation to be a prosecutor, not a persecutor. You are there merely 'to present the facts as interpreted by the prosecution'. Indeed, some experienced prosecutors open their cases with those very words. Prosecutors in England do not demand or even suggest swingeing sentences, and I am sorry that the prosecution now has a right of appeal against sentence, albeit a very limited one, because of the anguish it may cause to a defendant who has been leniently treated (and perhaps justly so).

On the other hand, there is no reason why the prosecutor should lean over backwards to help the defence with mitigation. If he overdoes this he may make himself unpopular with the defending advocate by stealing his thunder. There is, however, every reason for assisting the unrepresented defendant in this regard to the best of your ability.

Above all your attitude should be one of helpfulness to the court. You are not there to join battle with the judge or magistrates. They have a difficult task in sentencing—it is the most difficult aspect of their work—so do your best to help them to reach a solution at once just, and as favourable as reasonably possible to your client. There is no reason at all why you should not suggest an appropriate sentence, provided that you do it tactfully and that it is a sensible one and one to which you have given a good deal of thought; you must be able to defend your suggestion logically if challenged about it. It is no use suggesting a conditional discharge or a suspended sentence if the defendant is already the subject of a suspended sentence for a similar type of offence; and the fact that he has committed a different type of offence is usually no argument against the implementation of a suspended sentence, although it is often advanced as such by advocates. If they were right in this the law would be granting a licence to criminals to commit hundreds of different serious offences without real risk of losing their liberty, provided that they added variety to their criminal activities.

In making your suggestions be bold, realistic and firm. Don't use shy, sly phrases like: 'I invite you to take a certain course', to which I am afraid I used to rejoin with: 'Which way do you want me to go?' The options open to the sentencer are, fortunately, infinitely wider than they were twenty years ago. There is a real risk that the sentencer may forget one, the one most suited to your client, if you do not take the trouble to remind him of it. One day, as I went to lunch, I said to myself (of one of my regulars), 'Why didn't I think of the Day Training Centre for that chap?. That's the one thing that's never been tried, and I might have avoided prison for him that way.' His advocate had not reminded me of it. But still, there was soon another opportunity to try it out in the case of that particular defendant.

Do not forget, in appropriate cases—where your client has technically committed an offence but really no moral blame attaches to him—to recommend an absolute discharge. Some justices seem to think that this is tantamount to an acquittal. Be at pains to disabuse them of this idea.

This matter of pleas in mitigation is so important that I will devote the next few pages to specific matters to be looked for in all cases as possible mitigation (and one or two approaches to be avoided) most of which were propounded by a distinguished judge of great experience in criminal affairs, and my comments on those points.

Ten lamps of mitigation

Some years ago I invited Lord Dunboyne, who was to become the longest serving judge at the Inner London Crown Court, Newington Causeway, to address on the subject of sentencing a Law Group which I ran for Commonwealth law students at the (now, alas, defunct) British Council Student Centre. He devoted a substantial part of his address to the role of the advocate in sentencing, and especially to the plea in mitigation. He recommended the advocate to look for seven matters, which I will adopt here, adding three of my own. Whilst I kept a note of Lord Dunboyne's seven topics as headings, I did not note down his comments on them. So, having set out his headings and added my own, I will write comments upon each of them, but I should emphasise that they are my comments, not Lord Dunboyne's, although he has indicated that he does not disagree with them. Here is the list:

(1) Age.
(2) The defendant's domestic position.
(3) The defendant's work record and prospects.
(4) The possibility of justice being done by the imposition of a fine.
(5) Any period that the defendant has spent in custody awaiting trial or sentence.
(6) The defendant's own attitude.
(7) The special circumstances that led the defendant to commit this particular offence.
(8) Never imply that your client may not be guilty after all. Never indulge in the equivocal plea.
(9) Try to make your case different from all the other cases with which the court has to deal that day. Try to make it interesting.
(10) Never be pompous.

Comments

(1) *Age* This is relevant only with the young and old, and the Criminal Justice Act 1988, s 1(4) sets out detailed provisions relating to offenders under twenty-one. It is an unhappy fact that most (though by no means all) criminals come from broken homes, and judges recognise this, and make allowance for it. Being brought up in a children's home or other institution, however well run, is not the ideal training ground for life. But you should hesitate to use this argument beyond the age of about twenty-three. When I was told by an advocate that his client, aged forty, had had an unhappy childhood, I felt constrained to say that it was about time he got over it.

There is a gap between about twenty-three and sixty when age is irrelevant, but once people approach becoming 'senior citizens' they tend to get special concessions from the courts. No judge or magistrate that I know nowadays would willingly send a man or woman to prison if he felt that the defendant was likely to die during his sentence. The courts do not need to be reminded of this, beyond passing reference to the defendant's age. There is no need to 'wring the withers'.

It was not always thus. Sir Gerald Dodson was Recorder at the Old Bailey many years ago, yet still within my time, and he sentenced an old lag of seventy to seven years. 'Seven years!' exclaimed the aggrieved defendant, 'I shall never live to see the end of your sentence.' 'Never mind' said the judge quietly, 'just do as much as you can.' (He was the same judge who once addressed a defendant thus: 'Your learned counsel has produced a psychiatrist's report which has convinced me that you are suffering from schizophrenia. You are, as your learned counsel puts it, two persons. You will each of you go to prison for four years, consecutively.' Before calling psychiatrists or putting in their reports, as in all others aspects of mitigation, know your judge.)

(2) *Domestic position* Despite 'women's lib' there are still many more male convictions than female. Whether this is because women are naturally more law-abiding than men, or more cautious, or cleverer (so that they less often get caught) I have never been sure. But the fact remains that it is more often men that you will be defending, and it is their domestic position that you will usually be examining. I have already discussed the boy (and it applies equally to the girl) who comes from a broken home. But many offences are committed by men when their marriage, or a long-standing relationship with a woman (or nowadays occasionally with another man) breaks up. If this be so in your case, it is worth emphasising. A period of probation at a time of crisis can have a stabilising effect.

Likewise a good home background is worth mentioning, as obviously good home surroundings are less conducive to crime than the company and environment encountered in a detention centre or youth custody. But don't just repeat trite instructions like 'I am told he is a good boy at home'. When mothers said this to me about young tearaways committing offences in the early hours of the morning I was inclined to ask: 'Then why don't you keep him at home, madam?' And, please, never, never, indulge in the last dramatic gambit of the desperate advocate: 'Do you realise that it now costs £395 a week' (or whatever the current figure is; it seems to rise much faster even than the rate of inflation) 'to keep a man in prison?', to which I have been known to reply: 'Yes, and in the case of your client it will be worth every penny of it'. This type of advocacy is particularly unattractive. It savours of blackmail, and is either stupid or dishonest. It does not cost £395 a week (or whatever the figure is said to be) to keep a man in prison, although Mr Roy Hattersley once gave the Howard League some such figure. If you remove one man from prison all the normal expenses of the prison will continue; all the staff will still have to be paid, and the costs of administration, heating and lighting will all continue. Practically all that will be saved is the cost of the man's food and laundry, and I am quite sure that that comes nearer to £60 a week than £60 a day. So never mention this illusory financial factor in any court.

But the fact that a man has just married, or settled down with a woman in what is euphemistically but inaccurately described as 'a common law marriage' is relevant. (The fact that his girlfriend has recently become pregnant by him, if they are living apart, is not. It is surely not mitigation but aggravation that a young man who has chosen to get himself into trouble with the law should also have chosen to get a girl 'into trouble'—in the old fashioned sense of the term—and by his irresponsibility is bringing yet another ill-fated, underprivileged child into the world.) But many a young tearaway, who has committed almost every type of offence imaginable in his teens, has started to lead a criminally blameless life from the time that he has accepted the responsibility of setting up a home of his own with a partner. Women, I am convinced, are good for men. When I had a youngster before me who had committed all the conventional crimes bred of boredom in an affluent society, like taking and driving away, criminal damage when drunk, and trying out cannabis, I often felt like saying: 'You know, what you need is a good woman'—but I felt sure that I should be misunderstood!

(3) *Work record and work prospects* If someone is in

regular work which he has maintained for a long period, although he may have less excuse for a crime of dishonesty than an unemployed person, courts are very reluctant to disturb the useful pattern of his life, especially in days of high unemployment, and these factors should be strongly urged. Of course, they will not apply if he has stolen from his employers, and therefore been dismissed, and they may not apply if he has committed an offence serious in its social implications, like driving while disqualified, which always involves a deliberate flouting of an order of the court. Many courts consider imposing immediate imprisonment for this (it was mandatory to do so until not very long ago) so concentrate on urging the shortest possible sentence. I think that it is a pity that the shortest possible sentence is five days. Three, at a weekend, would be quite enough to deter many first offenders. But most employers would not deprive themselves of the services of a valued employee because of just a week's absence.

Make sure, though, that your client's account of his work is correct. A solicitor should discreetly check on this himself; if not, the court may do so. The probation officers at my court were dedicated to the defendants they tried to serve; but they were dedicated no less to the cause of justice, and they did not think that this was aided by the court being hoodwinked. When I felt suspicious about the defendant's protestations of having current employment, I asked the duty probation officer to ring up the firm concerned and ask to speak to the defendant (without, of course, revealing who was making the inquiry, or why). On far too many occasions the probation officer came back to report that the defendant had never been heard of at the firm, or that he worked there years ago but they had lost contact with him. Letters, too, indicating that a defendant is a hardworking and honest employee have occasionally to be treated with reserve: they may have been written by the defendant himself or by a helpful friend.

A forthcoming appearance in court is often an effective spur to the finding of gainful employment, but do beware of the unsubstantiated 'job to go to on Monday' syndrome. All courts have heard that one before. Some detailed enquiry about these prospects is required before they are advanced in mitigation. When a careless advocate told me a few years ago that one of my regular 'old lags' had a job as a roofer 'to start on Monday' I expressed some surprise that anyone would want their roof repaired on Christmas Day.

(4) *A fine or other non-custodial disposal rather than custody* Although the Home Office frequently tells us that this is the most effective way of disposing of cases, many of us who have the duty of writing off millions of pounds worth of uncollected fines every year have our doubts about this. Unfortunately the efficacy of fining has been greatly reduced by legislation introduced (at the suggestion of that same Home Office) preventing the court from backing up its fine with a suspended committal there and then when it has the defendant's means clearly in mind (except in the case of a defendant with 'no fixed abode in the United Kingdom'; this is a provision usually invoked against foreigners). On a recent visit to Tobago I noticed that, even in motoring cases, the stipendiary magistrate, when imposing a fine gave an alternative prison sentence, with a period, usually 48 hours, to pay. So contrary is this to our practice that I afterwards asked him why. 'Well', he said, 'if I didn't fix an alternative most of them would never pay, and so far as I know none of them has ever gone to prison for non-payment of one of my fines.' But such a pragmatic approach is discouraged in the English courts, which is why you may find the court reluctant to accept your suggestion that a fine would be appropriate. It should therefore be made usually just in the case of a man in employment and with 'a fixed abode'—if you are able to find out what that means—and where you are able realistically to put forward an offer of payment either immediately or within a specified time or by reasonable weekly instalments. A fine remains however the most sensible method of dealing with most of the less grave offences motivated by greed (such as shoplifting) and breaches of the road traffic laws.

Lord Dunboyne did not, in his address, mention compensation, which was much less in vogue then that it is now. One recent improvement in the law is that we have become much more concerned with the victims of crime. If your case is one in which compensation seems appropriate (this does not usually apply to damage or injury caused in road traffic accidents) and your client is in a position to pay it, make a realistic offer to the court. The defendant is unlikely to be in a position to pay compensation (much appreciated by the victim—especially the victim of an assault), if the court deprives him of his liberty. By making the defendant care for his victim the court can show that it, too, cares.

I must mention again the very important restrictions on incarceration contained in the Criminal Justice Act 1988, s 1(4) and subsequent legislation, especially in respect of offenders under twenty-one. They may well apply in your case, and yet the Bench may be so appalled by what the defendant has done that it is pushing these restrictions to the back of its mind and the advocate must then firmly but tactfully remind the court of what Parliament has decreed.

(5) *Time spent in custody* This is clearly most relevant in the case of a defendant who has been incarcerated for the first time. If it be the case, and it is very likely to be so, that your client's first period in custody has been a thoroughly unpleasant experience which may well in itself have brought him to his senses, so that no more loss of liberty is needed, emphasise this point. In the case of a serious first offence, calling for a prison sentence, the court may well see the logic of suspending that sentence if the defendant has already spent a little time in custody while reports were being prepared. The 'clanging of the prison gates' syndrome sounds over-dramatic, but many judges and magistrates recognise its effectiveness. The partially suspended sentence affords a new option to the sentencer. Recently a middle-aged man of previous good character had committed a quite serious burglary, and gone off to Germany in an effort to spend the proceeds, which he had succeeded in doing. He was arrested and charged on his return. He had no place to live in the United Kingdom,

and was remanded in custody for three weeks for reports. The gravity of the case was such that an immediate prison sentence was called for, and his advocate recognised this fact, but suggested that as the defendant had now undergone a custodial experience of three weeks and for the first time, a substantial part of the sentence could properly be suspended. When I suspended three-quarters of the six month sentence that I passed, the defendant, working out that he now had only just over a week to serve (allowing for the time spent in custody and for remission) looked pleased with me and even more pleased with his advocate.

(6) *The defendant's own attitude* This can be important to the sentencer, and often it is a good idea to use the defendant's own words. Courts are not very impressed to be told that a man of little education 'profoundly regrets his incursion into criminal activity and is thoroughly remorseful and wishes to make amends'. They would far rather hear that he himself has said: 'I must have been a nutter to have got mixed up in this when I had everything going for me'. But of course he must have said that for it to be quoted to the court. To make up something in the defendant's style would be grossly dishonest, and there is always the risk of a shout from the dock: ''Ere! I never said that'. Make sure too that your client's attitude is consistent with the expressions of regret that you are placing before the court. You cannot see what is going on behind you, but you would be disturbed if, as you waxed eloquent about your clients' sorrow and sense of shame, the three defendants just behind you were laughing and joking and nudging each other in the dock and asking: 'What's he on about?' (I have observed this situation on occasions.)

(7) *Special Circumstances* Because they will be special to the particular case, I cannot generalise about them, save to say that you should look to see if there was any immediate crisis in this defendant's life that caused him to commit this particular offence at this particular time. I still treasure a newspaper cutting of a case where I defended a woman on a charge of theft and forgery and obtaining goods by

deception. Charges of forgery in those days usually carried three years' imprisonment. The 'special circumstances' affecting this middle-aged lady of previous good character were that she had been deserted by her husband (she had become what nowadays is called 'a one parent family') her daughter had got a scholarship into a grammar school, the grammar school insisted on the wearing of a school uniform, she had no money for such a uniform, the local authority refused to pay for it, and the mother stole and forged a cheque simply to pay for this compulsory uniform so that her daughter should not be deprived of a good education. That grand old judge Mr Justice Cassels, then in his eighties, described the mother as 'the salt of the earth'. He gave her three years; but they were three years of probation.

(8) *Avoid the equivocal plea* One is used to defendants in person who plead guilty to dishonest handling and, in mitigation, say 'I'd never have touched it if I'd known it was hot'; used to defendants pleading guilty to drunk and disorderly and then saying 'But I wasn't drunk, of course. How could I be drunk when I'd only had half a pint of lager?' This is aggravating enough, as the whole proceedings then become abortive and have to be started again, but it is far more exasperating to hear from a trained advocate who has allowed his client to plead guilty to a charge of shoplifting: 'She instructs me to say that she is very sorry that she forgot to pay'. Complaint is sometimes made that some justices do not seem to know the difference between absentmindedness and theft. It is quite unforgivable when the advocate appears unaware of this distinction by advancing this sort of mitigation (which I have heard done, happily rarely). Or is the advocate just trying to have the best of both worlds?

(9) *Make it interesting* Judges and magistrates are sometimes criticised for appearing bored, even somnolent. But pity the poor Bench that has to listen to this sort of thing twenty times day (and in a busy Crown Court or

magistrates' court a workload of twenty pleas in mitigation is not unusual):

'The defendant in this case is very sorry for what he has done. It was the drink that made him do it, and he's promised to cut down on his drinking. He's pleaded guilty and was co-operative with the police. I've spoken to his mother who says that he is a good boy at home and his long criminal record is all due to the bad company he keeps, as he is easily led. He's asking for one last chance because he's just learned that his girlfriend has become pregnant. He's very proud to learn that he is about to become a father, and although he's been unemployed for a long time, he's got a job to start on Monday. Don't forget that if you send him to prison it will cost the taxpayer £395 a week and his girlfriend will have to draw social security.'

As this trite and turgid stuff is churned out one feels that this mitigation is this advocate's Mark III model. He has two other slight variations for other occasions (where for instance the defendant is too old to impregnate anybody). And, as the day wears on, so does the court. Then an advocate rises alertly to his feet and with his first words revives the Bench's flagging spirits: 'Sir, this is a most unusual case and I'm going to ask you to take a most unusual course.' Eyes and minds are opened because at least the advocate is trying to be interesting.

(10) *Pomposity* This vice exists more in young barristers than in young solicitors. It is a most unattractive quality, being akin to arrogance. When an advocate is being pompous, there is an almost irresistable urge to deflate him. A barrister once addressed me in these terms when pleading guilty on behalf of a medical practitioner to careless driving:

'May it please you, sir, my client, who is an Indian doctor of the utmost respectability, approached these crossroads travelling at a moderate speed upon the minor road t'wards the major road, but alas!—and herein lies the reason for his tendering upon my advice, which I hope in all the circumstances you will feel was proper advice, a plea of guilty to this charge—alas! he failed to observe the presence upon the major road of the other vehicle until just before "le moment critique". Sir, I hand in his licence, which you will find is a virgin.'

In the first edition of this book I indicated that for reasons of delicacy I would not record my riposte to this pompous verbiage, but so many students and others have asked me to do so that I will include it now.

In those days we still put errant motorists in the dock, and after his counsel's plea in mitigation the medical man stood there trembling and perhaps wondering if we still had the death penalty for careless driving in this country. I looked at him very severely and addressed him in these terms: 'You, as a doctor, will surely realise that as a virgin approaches "le moment critique" she must proceed with the utmost caution. This you failed to do, and you will pay a fine of £5 . . .'

(11) *The defendant's plea of guilty* At the risk of inelegance I must add an eleventh player to my team, for in the last few years it has become established law that, generally speaking, there should be a discount of between a fifth and a third for a plea of guilty. (By a process of 'double-think' of which only lawyers are capable, a defendant does not get more for exercising his rights and fighting a case, but he does get less for 'putting his hand up'). In most instances it is worth reminding the court of the plea of guilty, and whilst all the cases from which this principle derives have involved immediate sentences of imprisonment (not many other sentences find their way into the Court of Appeal), there is no reason why it should not apply equally to suspended sentences, fines and Community Service and Attendance Centre Orders. I used the expressions 'generally speaking' and 'in most instances' because the discount rule does not invariably apply. If the main thrust of your argument has been to persuade a bench of magistrates not to commit an old lag for sentence, it would not be appropriate to ask them to impose a sentence of less than six months; likewise, if your main concern is that any sentence of imprisonment shall be suspended,

you will not be too worried, if you succeed, by the length of that period of custody. Clearly a defendant who has owned up to his offence from the word 'Go'-or rather the word 'Stop'-is in a stronger position to 'qualify' for a substantial discount than the accused whose first intimation of his plea comes at the door of the court which has set aside time for the trial of his case, especially if, for example, he has maintained his plea of Not Guilty in the belief that the main prosecution witness in, say, a robbery case, would not be brought back from abroad to testify and, contrary to his expectations, the complainant turns up. But, subject to these few exceptions, the discount principle is now well established and worth emphasising.

5 Dress and modes of address

While at the Bar I once had to defend, before the late Mr R E Seaton, then Chairman of London Sessions, and a jury, an American airman charged with dealing in uncustomed liquor. Forty litre bottles of Bourbon had been found in the boot of his car as he drove towards the clubs of the West End of London. His defence was that he was on his way to a party, and to explain the possession of this formidable amount of alcohol, he desired to call a sort of 'expert witness', an American staff-sergeant who would depose to the drinking habits of American servicemen. Unfortunately the trial had to be delayed while my instructing solicitor sought out the missing witness, who was increasing his expertise in a nearby hostelry, and his arrival coincided with a complete change of atmosphere in Court No 1 of London Sessions, which almost immediately came to resemble that of a four-ale bar.

'Is your name Chuck Drinkwater?' I asked (improbably).

'Sure, your Grace', came the reply.

'And are you a staff-sergeant in the United States Forces?'

'That's right, your Grace.'

Mr Seaton could stand it no longer. 'In this country', he pointed out, 'only Dukes and Archbishops are addressed as "Your Grace", and Mr Crowther happens to be neither.'

'Oh, is that so, your Honour?' asked the witness in surprise, speaking to a judge who was accustomed to being addressed as 'My Lord'.

In fact, the American showed remarkable prescience, for, while I am unlikely ever to become either a Duke or an Archbishop, Mr Seaton's successors, since the Courts Act

1971 the Crown Court judges, have all, with a few exceptions, been addressed as 'Your Honour', a title previously reserved for county court judges and official referees.

But the great moment of that case occurred a little later when Mr Seaton ventured upon a further sardonic intervention:

'But Mr Drinkwater', he said, 'we have been told by the defendant that there were to be about twenty people at this party and there were forty litres of whiskey found in the boot of his car. You as an expert are surely not suggesting that that would be an appropriate amount to be drunk by twenty people in one night?'

'Gee, Judge', commented the witness, 'I guess you never been to an American party.'

'May it please your Lordship in this case I appear for the plaintiff, and the defendant is represented by learned friend Mr Guinea-brief.' This is the correct way for a barrister to open a civil case before a High Court judge, and he should seek if at all possible never to use the first person singular again during the currency of the case (*see* Chapter 1). It is open to all sorts of permutations according to the nature and sex of the tribunal, and, indeed the professional status of the defence advocate. If he or she is a barrister it is customary to refer to the opponent as 'my learned friend'; if a solicitor as 'my friend'. Having had as many solicitors as counsel appearing before me I can see no justification for the subtle innuendo arising from this distinction.

'Your Lordship(s)' and 'My Lord(s)' are the appropriate forms of address for members of the House of Lords, the Court of Appeal, and all High Court judges, including special commissioners sitting temporarily in the High Court; also for any person trying cases at the Central Criminal Court (Old Bailey) in whatever capacity; also, according to a directive given by the then Lord Chief Justice on 22 December 1971 to any judge who nine days later would be Recorder of Liverpool or Manchester.

The correct form of address for the House of Lords may

not be an immediate problem for the beginner at the Bar, but I will optimistically include it. The House of Lords sitting in a judicial capacity should be referred to as 'Your Lordships' House' (never as 'a court'); and do not forget that the reasoning of their Lordships appears in their 'speeches'—never their 'judgments'.

Moving down a little, if in the Court of Appeal you are referring to a judgment of a member of that august body and he is present, do it in this way: 'It is as my Lord Justice Lawton has just said', or if he is not present, 'as the Lord Justice Lawton said in the case of *Parrot* v *Bullfinch*'. (Never refer to Lawton LJ or Denning MR. *Always* avoid the use of initials in court.)

In addressing the judge call him, vocatively, 'My Lord', or using the third person form of address 'Your Lordship'. (This is equivalent to the polite form of address in Spanish, *Usted*, which is really a contraction of *Vuestra Merced* (your mercy)—more appropriate, perhaps, to magistrates.)

The expression 'If Your Lordship (or Your Honour) pleases' is an extraordinarily useful mode of retreat from a line of argument that you realise to be no longer tenable. You have been arguing away at a proposition: the judge gets weary and points out a flaw in it. 'If your Lordship pleases' indicates to him that you realise you have made a fool of yourself, while your client feels that you are just exchanging pleasantries with the judge. Please pronounce 'My Lord' as 'My Lord'. The contraction used by some elderly barristers of 'Me Lud', sounds rather like some low class hostelry.

When you appear before a permanent judge in any Crown Court other than the Old Bailey (and with the very limited exceptions in respect of Manchester and Liverpool already mentioned) or any county court or before one of the few official referees, you should, since 1 January 1972, address him or her as 'Your Honour'. Save where a High Court judge is trying the case, or where a registrar is dealing with the matter, judges determining divorce issues are now referred to as 'Your Honour'. This form of appellation, quite rare a little more than two decades ago, is now one of the most usual. It should also be used to address recorders—the recorders who leave their practices as barristers or solicitors to sit in the Crown Courts for a minimum of four weeks per year—and Deputy Circuit Judges.

Most persons sitting in a judicial or quasi-judicial capacity other than those already mentioned should be called 'Sir' or 'Madam': registrars of the Family Division and of the county courts; coroners, stipendiary magistrates, chairmen of lay benches, chairmen of statutory tribunals, etc. Lord Denning used to sit as a lay justice. If you found that he was chairman of the Bench—and once I appeared before a bench of lay justices presided over by a formidable Chancery judge (a most traumatic experience, I can assure you!)—you should address him as 'Sir'. It is the capacity in which he is currently adjudicating, not his more elevated position, that is relevant.

Traditionally solicitors address magistrates, lay and stipendiary, as 'Your Worship(s)'. (Police officers tend to corrupt this into 'Your Wash-Ups'.) This is, as I have said, the English equivalent of the polite third person form of address *Usted(es) Merced(es)* in Spanish. But a barrister never does so: for him it is always 'Sir' or 'Madam', according to the sex of the chairman. The reason for this in the case of stipendiary magistrates is clear. Until 1964 all stipendiary magistrates had come from the Bar (now there are several ex-solicitors in this office) and 'we are all equal at the Bar'. 'Sir' or 'Madam' is a mark of respect that can properly be employed in addressing any person who is one's equal. Lay justices, of course, have not (save in a few cases) come from the Bar, but presumably it is appropriate to address them in the same way, because they hold their honorary and honourable office by virtue of being ladies and gentlemen of merit in the community.

With a plural Bench (such as a Bench of lay justices, who may be dealing with criminal, matrimonial, juvenile or licensing matters) if you are a barrister and have the duty of opening begin by saying:

'May it please you sir (or madam) and members of the Bench, I appear for the Crown Prosecution Service (or the complainant).' Remember that the other members of the

Bench have equal voting rights with the chairman, so include them all in order to influence them all. As a solicitor you will say 'Your Worships', a term that is all-embracing, so this problem does not arise so acutely. Thereafter address the Chairman ('Sir' or 'Madam' or 'Your Worship'), but do not forget to look at the other members of the Bench, attracting their attention (or, at least, their sympathy).

An exception to the 'Sir' or 'Madam' rule when appearing before those holding junior judicial office arises in the case of Masters of the Queen's Bench or Chancery Divisions, who are always addressed as 'Master' (which sounds a bit like a religious innovation). So far no ladies hold this office, which is perhaps just as well, since it might lead to insuperable difficulties of nomenclature.

The advent of women to high judicial office is comparatively recent. When Rose Heilbron QC became a chairman of Quarter Sessions at Burnley about a quarter of a century ago, nobody knew quite how to address her. Rumour has it that the problem was resolved by the first defendant who appeared before her, to whom she showed great clemency, and who responded with 'Thank you, My Fair Lady'.

Now, of course, she is one of several female High Court judges. Although initially they were referred to as 'My Lord', this was soon recognised as being rather artificial, and the correct appellation now is 'My Lady'. But Elizabeth Butler-Sloss, the first lady to sit in the Court of Appeal, calls herself—Lord Justice Butler-Sloss.

Try to get it right. It is more pleasing to the tribunal to be correctly addressed. Some of my drunks used to address me as 'Your Majesty', but I usually responded with: 'Flattery will get you nowhere, Mr O'Sullivan'.

How often should you use the appellation? If you use it too little you sound abrupt and discourteous; if too much, fawning and servile. An old advertisement for a shaving stick, before electric razors (and beards) became so popular, provided the answer: 'Not too little, not too much—but just right'.

If you meet a judge socially, or bump into him in Chancery Lane, greet him as 'Judge'—not 'My Lord' or

'Your Honour'—unless he be a Lord Justice of Appeal in which case it is 'Lord Justice', or a Lord of Appeal in Ordinary, in which case 'Lord Scarman', or whoever he is. But may I advise against the practice of a young barrister friend of mine, in the days when work at the Bar was hard to come by, of greeting everybody he saw wearing a dark suit in the Temple with the words: 'Good afternoon, Judge'? None of the solicitors' clerks thus addressed ever sent him a brief.

We have discussed at length how the judges and magistrates should be addressed or referred to in and out of court. What about the persons facing criminal charges? Not so long ago they were almost always spoken of as 'the prisoners'. This seems to me to be an expression redolent with anticipatory prejudice. A very competent defending solicitor advocate who frequently appeared before me invariably rose to say. 'I appear for the accused man' ('invariably' because I never remember him appearing for a woman accused of an offence—after reading this he started referring to his client as 'the accused person'). This is certainly preferable to 'the prisoner'. But surely the best—because the most neutral—of all expressions is 'the defendant'.

If you want to add variety to your presentation of the case by ringing the changes you can, of course, refer to the defendant by name. How? 'Sykes who is accused of burglary' 'Bill Sykes', 'Mr Sykes', or just plain 'Bill'? Lord Goddard's policy was to say 'Mr Sykes' until conviction, after which the form of appellation changed to 'Sykes'. With all due respect to a very great Lord Chief Justice I beg to differ. The fact that a person is about to be robbed of his or her liberty (or money) is surely not a reason for him or her to be deprived also of dignity. 'Mr Sykes' or 'Miss Sykes' throughout the proceedings is much to be preferred to 'Sykes', whether you are examining-in-chief or cross-examining (or judging). 'Bill' is mandatory in the relaxed atmosphere of the juvenile courts (where a lot of the most serious crime is dealt with nowadays) but wholly inappropriate in the adult courts. It savours of an all too familiar relationship between the advocate and the defendant, and must be eschewed at all costs.

I wish to say less on the subject of dress in court than on modes of address. Whilst it is obvious that gowns (and wigs in the case of barristers) are still worn in the High Court and above and in the Crown Court and county court but not in the magistrates' court, perhaps it is helpful to point out that they are to be worn before Courts-Martial and are not generally worn when appearing in chambers—before a judge, a master or a registrar; nor are they worn before statutory tribunals. As to the robes themselves, make sure they are smart and clean and carried well—except for the barrister's wig, which, if acquired new, should be kicked around a dirty floor for ten minutes before being worn. I need not say much of the style of dress to be worn by advocates, male and female, as this subject was dealt with generally by my friend and former colleague Ronald Bartle, the Bow Street magistrate, in an article which appeared at 146 JPN 246 (1982). The Bar Council has laid down rules of etiquette for the attire of barristers in all courts and, if they follow these rules, they will not go wrong. I do not think that there are any such regulations governing solicitors, but, as one who is not particularly concerned with sartorical elegance, my advice to all advocates would simply be: dress soberly in court. You should be prepared to do this as a mark of respect for the court of which you are a part. Even if you do not see it in that way, at least dress sensibly out of consideration for the feelings of your client. In April 1990 a solicitor conducting a case in a white suit and white shoes was rebuked by a magistrate, and the Law Society upheld the complaint. Clothes worn in court, they said, should be 'suitable and unobtrusive'

I had a very illustrious predecessor at West London who will never be forgotten by those who appeared before him (including myself). I well recall one Saturday afternoon on which he refused to hear a solicitor because he had observed that he was wearing brown suede shoes. ('I cannot see you', he declared, 'your footwear is more suitable for the golf course than for a court of law'.) That solicitor did not serve his client well by arousing needlessly that magistrate's ire and causing an unnecessary adjournment and further costs.

Whilst I myself would never have reacted in that way, I did not like advocates to address the court with a hand or hands in pocket(s). It all seemed to me most unfair. The nervous defendant comes to take the oath and the usher has his big moment and bellows: 'Take your hand out of your pocket when you're addressing the magistrate' (causing the defendant to forget most of what he wanted to say in evidence). The solicitor or barrister rises and, with hand in pocket (and perhaps even with a foot on the bench) asks: 'Are you Bert Bloggins?' If the magistrate says nothing, it looks as though there is one law for the rich and one for the poor, so I usually intervened to ask the advocate: 'Would *you* be equally comfortable with your hand out of your pocket?' Most advocates responded immediately and as I wished but I must confess to having been a little surprised one morning by a young barrister who answered: 'No, I would not, I always address all courts with my hands in my pockets and I see no reason to make an exception in yours'.

It took me a few seconds to recover, but when I had done so I replied: 'I am afraid you are trying to show off, and I am anxious that you should do so before the smallest possible audience. I will take your case at half past four'— which I did.

He appeared before me many times thereafter, and I never again saw his hand in his pocket and, in fairness to him, I think that I should say that having grown out of his youthful arrogance he became a really good advocate.

The most amusing book on the law that I have ever read is *Smugglers' Circuit* by Sir Denys Roberts, the popular former Chief Justice of Hong Kong, written in his early days at the Bar in England. A passage in that delightful book (published by Methuen in 1954) describing a most curious trial reads as follows:

> 'The Judge took his seat at half-past ten next morning. "I must warn both counsel that I have to travel today,

as this is the Commission Day for Crancester, so I cannot sit beyond one o'clock." At the point the Judge noticed that something was wrong. Humphrey was sitting on counsel's bench, dressed in a tartan sports jacket, dove-grey corduroy trousers, green shirt and a scarlet tie. The Judge closed his eyes, convinced that this was the first twinge of another attack of migraine. When he opened them the same startling picture met his eyes, being now further emphasised by a glimpse of a sand-coloured suede shoe and a yellow sock poking round the corner of the bench.

As the Judge leaned forward to ask the Clerk whether he had seen it too, the latter called on the case.

"Proudfoot and Banting, part heard."

Before the Judge could say anything, Gina had risen and began her final speech for the defence. "If it please your Lordship I shall not detain the Court very long in my address, since in my submission the evidence . . ."

The Judge tore his eyes away from Humphrey and looked at Gina for the first time. Gina was even more inappropriately garbed. Her light summer dress of brilliant colours may have been designed for coolness, but it could equally well serve far less reputable ends. Her arms and shoulders were completely bare, and the dress was moulded closely to her chest, which it covered with very little to spare. Her nakedness was further accentuated by a plunging neckline which ran recklessly downwards. The Judge could not see her back, but was sure that, if she turned, he would be able to count separately, and in detail, each and every bone of her spine from top to bottom, using the word in its fullest sense. Gina's make up, though in subdued colours, was heavier than was usual for a woman barrister in Court. On her head was a hat of unmistakable frivolity.

"Miss Lasalle", thundered the Judge, "I cannot see you." '

6 Opening and closing speeches

In the previous chapter I recommended that you should, if acting for the prosecution or the complainant in a magistrates' court, begin with the words: 'May it please you Sir (or Madam), in this case I appear for the Crown Prosecution Service (or the complainant) and the defendant (or the respondent) is represented by my learned friend, Mr Guinea-Brief'. 'But who are YOU?' asked a justice the other day. 'We would like to know who is prosecuting in the case. It's so embarrassing to wish to ask the advocate a question and not to know his or her name, especially if they've forgotten to fill in the slip; or if the board with details of the advocates has gone missing.' It's a valid point, so, unless you are well-known (or notorious) in that court, introduce yourself also by adding, after 'I appear for the prosecution' the words 'and my name is Weepers' (not 'Mr Weepers' or 'Miss Weepers' or 'Willie Weepers', etc—just plain 'Weepers') before introducing your opponent. There will then follow your opening speech (if any). I will not presume to comment on the sort of speeches that might move the House of Lords or the Privy Council or the Court of Appeal or the Divisional Court, as I feel that those who regularly practise there will have little need of my advice. But I will mention opening addresses in High Court actions and jury trials.

In the High Court, counsel for the plaintiff should first state what the nature of the case is ('My Lord, this is an action for damages for personal injuries arising from the alleged negligence of the defendant') followed by a brief narrative of the events leading up to the proceedings being launched, delivered preferably in chronological order. (Lord Denning tells of an advocate who always presented his cases in a state of great confusion, until one very weary judge said that he really must stipulate for some sort of order. 'There are so many to choose from . . . Even the alphabetical would be better than no order at all!') Then it is the duty of the opening advocate to read the pleadings, sounding equally enthusiastic (well, almost equally enthusiastic!) when he reads out the defence as when he recites the statement of claim. Thereafter there will probably be an agreed bundle of correspondence to be read (or, rather, skimmed through). The judge will not want you to read out: 'We thank you for yours of the 13th ult, to which we will reply as soon as possible. Your faithfully.' This requires careful editing, deleting all that is not relevant, but making sure that you are completely fair to the other side, by neither omitting anything in the correspondence favourable to them, nor anything unfavourable to your own case. (The American attorney whom I mentioned in an earlier chapter expressed surprise that each side did not insist on reading its own letters, but that is really not necessary under our system.) Then refer the judge briefly to any relevant statute or case law. You should have given the usher your list of authorities before the case began, so that they will be up on the judge's bench, ready for him to refer to them. You yourself will argue them in greater depth in the light of the evidence, when it comes to your closing address. You should also have told your opponent of any authorities to which you wish to refer, and also of any of which you are aware that are adverse to your case. You have no special property in them because you have discovered them, and your primary duty to the court and to your profession is that justice should be done, not that you should win.

Finally summarise very briefly why you say, on the law and the facts, that at the end of the day the verdict should go in your favour.

The procedure for advocates (both solicitors and barristers) in the county courts is similar, except that here we have 'particulars of claim' instead of the statement of claim, and you should be much more concise in your address. The county court judge may have six contested cases that day and he would like to get through them. The High Court judge will start his next case when he finishes yours. I once apologised to Henry Elam, the ever-patient and courteous Deputy Chairman of London Sessions, for taking what I thought had been an inordinately long time over an appeal. 'Don't you worry, Mr Crowther', he said, soothingly. 'If I were not trying your case, I'd be trying another.' It seemed a benign philosophy.

For many years I advised on Wednesday evenings at Toynbee Hall Legal Advice Centre, in London's East End. I had distinguished predecessors in Lord Justice Birkett and Sir Frank Milton. In those days we used to conduct cases for clients in court, for a nominal two guineas, or free, if they could afford nothing.

One evening a very sad Austrian refugee came in. This was his story. He had been the tenant of a flat in Stepney. He had sub-let a room there for £1 a week to a Maltese. All had gone well until the Austrian had been taken into hospital suffering from mental illness (and there were times when we felt that his release had been premature). After several years he came out and returned to his home. The locks had been changed, but eventually the Maltese had answered his repeated knocking. 'Who are you?' the Maltese had demanded. 'I am your landlord', replied the Austrian. 'Go away' shouted the Maltese, 'I have never seen you before in my life. You must be mad. Go away, or I will knock you down.'

The Austrian may have been mad, but he was sane enough to realise that discretion is the better part of valour, and he withdrew and came to see us. We wrote to the Maltese; no reply. We wrote to the head landlords. They replied that the Austrian had forfeited his tenancy by illegally letting to the Maltese, whom they much preferred as a tenant anyway. It was obvious that the Austrian was not going to get his home back. But all his furniture and personal belongings were there, so we wrote to the Maltese asking him to surrender these. We received no reply.

In due course an action was launched and the parties

appeared in the Shoreditch County Court, I appearing for the Austrian. My opening address went something like this:

'May it please your Honour, in this case I appear for the plaintiff and the defendant is not represented' (I did not have to introduce myself as my name appeared at the foot of the particulars of claim). 'Your Honour, this is an action in detinue. Five years ago the plaintiff let a room in his flat to the defendant and both lived there quite amicably for a year or more. Then the plaintiff became ill and had to have prolonged treatment in hospital. After his return home the defendant, who in the meantime had assumed occupation of the whole flat, refused to recognise or acknowledge the plaintiff and indeed threatened him. The plaintiff is not now seeking to recover the flat, but he left there numerous personal possessions which the defendant refuses to give up. These are set out in the schedule to the particulars of claim which, with your Honour's leave, I will now read:

'The defendant unlawfully detained and detains numerous items belonging to the plaintiff as set out in the schedule hereto. The plaintiff demanded the return of the aforesaid items by letter dated 1 April 1955 but the defendant has wrongfully refused and/or failed to deliver up the same.

'May I now refer your Honour to that letter, since your Honour will know that as a matter of law there must be a demand in writing for the return of the goods before proceedings are commenced? There has been notice to produce, your Honour, so I will call for the original before producing a copy, and then call the plaintiff to give evidence.'

It was only at that point that things started to go seriously wrong. Although the Austrian had lived in England for about twenty years he spoke little English. Until I met him I thought I understood German. But at that time I had an Austrian girlfriend, so, as she seemed perfect in every other respect, I thought she would be the ideal person to interpret. This would have two advantages: her services would be free, and she would see me in action—in a case that I believed to be unlosable. (This is why I remember the details of this case so well.) Unfortunately she did not understand the plaintiff either. He was speaking, she said, a mixture of Yiddish and an obscure Viennese dialect that had been obsolete since the end of the First World War! And when I called upon the defendant to produce the letter, it was obvious that he did not understand English either. (How they, the parties, had had the conversation that I quoted earlier I shall never know!) And this was the day that the sixth form of the local girls' school had come to the Shoreditch County Court to watch English justice at work . . . It was yet another example of the golden rule that I mentioned in the first chapter that you should never take your friends or relations to watch your performance in court.

With a jury it is rather different. Matters have to be explained more slowly and in greater detail. The law has to be spelt out in simple language. It is customary—and right—for prosecuting counsel to explain both the burden and standard of proof in opening a criminal case, although I have known some criminal judges who have felt this to be 'molly-coddling' the defendant, and that it is a matter that can safely be left to defence counsel to elaborate on, and to the judge to refer to (just once). But do not underestimate the jury. Ther may be some shrewd common sense among them. They will not welcome being talked down to in a condescending or patronising manner. Even so, Lewis Carroll's observation 'If I say a thing three times, it must be true', has more application to trial by jury than to trial by judge alone.

Some years ago I heard a talk on advocacy given by one of the then greatest Queen's Counsel, Michael Eastham—later a High Court judge—to Bar students of Lincoln's Inn. He sought to draw a distinction between conducting a case before a judge and jury and before a judge alone. (In those days there were many more civil actions tried by juries than now. One even had juries—of eight persons—in county courts. Nowadays it is rare for any civil matters other than libel and slander and false imprisonment and malicious prosecution to be tried by jury. Lord Atkin's prediction, that the English civil jury (which de Tocquevile had regarded as 'the foundation of English civil liberty') would soon be 'as rare as the black swan', has come true. Even so, I believe that Mr Justice Eastham's observations still have some relevance and validity.)

For speeches to a judge sitting alone, Mr Justice Eastham advocated six rules:

(1) DON'T treat him as a jury, ie don't labour the obvious, and don't get too passionate or emotional. Lord Denning tells a lovely story about this. Martin O'Connor, he recalls, was a very flamboyant Irish advocate, given to flights of rhetoric. He was appearing before the blunt, dour Mr Justice Swift. Three times the judge interrupted the flow of passionate oratory to say 'There's no jury in this case, Mr O'Connor'. But the advocate's natural propensity for drama got the better of him once again. Mr Justice Swift tapped that formidable pencil on the bench before him, but now he was to address someone else: 'Usher, switch on the light over the jury box. Mr O'Connor doesn't believe me.'

(2) DON'T open your case in too much detail to the judge—certainly do so in less detail than you would with a jury. Also, I would repeat, never open 'too high', ie on a note indicating over-confidence in your cause. The judge (or the jury) has to determine the case on the evidence, and the witnesses may let you down. Save your enthusiasm for your closing speech.

(3) DON'T make the same point more than once to a judge. The chances are that he will get it first time.

(4) DON'T in your speeches try to please the person for whom you are appearing; only try to help the judge.

(5) DO be selective in your argument. You don't have to throw every point in. Indeed, be selective according to the idiosyncracies of the judge. There was a delightfully warmhearted judge called Tudor Rees in Surrey years ago. I was appearing for the tenant in a Rent Act case. His landlords wanted the house in which he and his family were living and had offered them a flat instead. The issue was whether this was 'suitable alternative accommodation'. The nature and frequency of the judge's interruptions of

my closing speech indicated clearly to me that I was losing. Suddenly I remembered seeing a little snippet in the *Evening Standard* a few nights before of a dictum of this judge, a great animal lover. 'If there are no dogs in heaven', he had said, 'I do not wish to go there.' (I hope there are dogs in heaven, for the late Judge Tudor Rees richly deserves a place in the Elysian Fields.) I turned to the defendant: 'Have you got a dog?' I asked. 'Yes, why?' he exclaimed, loking at me as though I were completely mad. But I was back addressing the judge: 'And then, your Honour, there's the question of the dog. The dog would never be happy in this flat, with no garden, no trees . . .' The judge's face brightened: 'Oh, there's a dog is there?' he smiled, 'I didn't realise there was a dog. A dog is a member of an English family and as such is entitled to be considered. This flat would be quite unsuitable for the dog. I shall certainly not make an order.'

(6) DO be courteous. Rudeness, abrasiveness, bullying are quite out of place in any court. Some of the most courteous advocates I have been against have been the most deadly. I would put the late Lord Justice Sebag Shaw in this category. After the famous Dr Adams' murder trial in 1957, *The Times* commented that never once during that protracted case did defending counsel, Geoffrey Lawrence QC (afterwards a High Court judge) raise his voice. This is how Geoffrey Lawrence dealt with the burden of proof in his closing address to the jury. Note the cadence in his submissions:

> 'Justice is of paramount consideration here, and the only way in which this can be done is for you to judge the matter on what you have heard in this court and in this court only.
>
> What you read in the papers, what you hear in the train, what you hear in the cafés and restaurants, what your friends and relations come and tell you; rumour, gossip, all the rest of it, may be so wrong.
>
> The possibility of guilt is not enough, suspicion is not enough, probability is not enough, likelihood is not.

A criminal matter is not a question of balancing probabilities and deciding in favour of a probability.

If the accusation is not proved beyond reasonable doubt against the man accused in the dock, then by law he is entitled to be acquitted, because that is the way our rules work. It is no concession to give him the benefit of the doubt. He is entitled by law to a verdict of not guilty.'

Lawrence had taken the bold decision not to call Dr Adams to give evidence. Nevertheless, the defendant was acquitted of murder by the jury after only a short retirement. Some part of the credit for this result must be attributed to counsel's thorough and penetrating closing speech.

If your speeches be sensitive to the atmosphere of the court. If the judge appears to be wearying of your eloquence, abbreviate it. There is a good example of such flexibility in Sir Deny Roberts delightful book *Smugglers' Circuit* to which I have referred to in the previous chapter. The judge had studied the pleadings before sitting and he did not think much of the case he had to try.

' "I warn you both", he said fiercely, "that I shall confine this case very closely to the pleadings, so that no more time shall be wasted than is unavoidable. Now, Mr Crichton."

Humphrey picked up the paper on which he had so painstakingly written out his opening speech, and started off.

"The plaintiff who is a retired army officer of unimpeachable reputation entered the *Rose and Crown* in Bettingford on the evening of 14th April of this year."

"I don't want to hear all this, Mr Crichton."

"But, My Lord, I'm opening."

"I am aware of that. I was merely intimating that I considered it superfluous."

"I thought it might make matters clearer to your Lordship if I . . ."

"Matters are quite clear to me, Mr Crichton. I hope you are not making the mistake, made by so many of your contemporaries, of assuming that everything has to be explained to a Judge, not only in words of one syllable, but twice, and slowly."

"As your Lordship pleases," replied Humphrey. "I will call the evidence before your Lordship straight away." '

What a useful phrase 'As your Lordship pleases' is for a dignified retreat from a position recognised as being no longer tenable!

As to magistrates' courts, remember that you have the right to make only one speech (unless there is a point of law for argument in rebuttal at the end of the case) and if you are for the prosecution or complainant your speech will come at the beginning or not at all. Even so, do not open before a stipendiary, subject as he is to the tyranny of the daily list, unless the case you are prosecuting contains some point of law with which you think he may be unfamiliar or is of exceptional complexity. Likewise lay justices will not be pleased by an opening of an ordinary shop-lifting case or a simple careless driving, but they might welcome your drawing their attention to the salient points of something a little more complicated.

The sort of case in which an explanatory opening might be welcome to lay justices was a matrimonial case in which I appeared before the Bromley Bench many years ago. The allegation was one of persistent cruelty, founded on a bus driver's spending far more time than his normal working hours with his regular (or irregular?) conductress—there was a great deal of unpaid overtime in this case—as a result of which his poor wife's health had suffered. I thought it right to open this one: to point out that as a matter of law unproved but reasonably suspected adultery could constitute cruelty if there were injury to health in consequence, just as much as unfounded allegations of adultery could do so.

Speeches to juries are usually more colourful and couched in more literary language than those to judges and magistrates, who are often quite pleased when the advocate says: 'There are just four points that I want to make in closing'. If you do this before a Bench of justices, the chances are that one of them will write down your four (or however many) points, and he or she will be arguing them for you when the justices get into the retiring room.

I never found the late Judge Clothier at Lambeth County Court a sympathetic judge before whom to appear, and I lost most of my cases before him. But then I had a long, complicated and important case there which had lasted two and a half days and I seemed to be winning. My opponent made his closing speech on the third morning to the accompaniment of a good deal of heckling from the judge, and I felt sure that I was on to a good thing. My opponent sat down, exhausted, at about 1 pm and, as I thought I had won and wanted to get away to do another case elswhere I said to the judge: 'I wonder if your Honour would mind if I left my pupil here this afternoon. I don't imagine your Honour will wish to hear me, in view of the comments that you have made on the defence case.'

'You can do what you like,' said the judge abruptly, 'but I warn you that I'm against you at the moment.'

I had no lunch that day, and it was an hour of the most concentrated work that I had ever done. As I had been sure throughout that I was winning, I had mistakenly not prepared a closing speech, so all that I could do was to enumerate the points in the plaintiff's favour. There were thirteen of them. The judge looked sceptical about the first ten. Number eleven went as follows: 'Your Honour will see that in the original defence, filed by the defendant in person before he had the benefit of legal advice, he used the word "suggested", but when an amended defence was filed by my learned friend the word "suggested" was changed to "requested".'

'Ah, I hadn't noticed that', said the judge. 'It makes all the difference to this case. I needn't trouble you further.' So I won the case (and lost the other brief—and the other solicitor too, as it was his son I was supposed to be defending in another court). Contrary to popular belief cases are sometimes won on speeches, if the advocate can pick out points that the Bench may have missed.

All the way through the case you must be alert to everything that is going on. Your eyes and ears must always be open. It is essential that you develop the facility for making neat legible notes for incorporation in your closing speech, which, in a magistrates' court, you will usually have no time to prepare. In a stipendiary court the magistrate will often interrupt to argue with you, so you must be prepared for a dialogue, but this seldom happens with lay justices. You are entitled to comment on the demeanour of witnesses—but be sure of your ground before you do so. As I emphasised in the first chapter, you must never express your personal opinions in court. It is most improper to do so. Such expressions as 'I think', 'I believe', or 'in my view' are wholly inappropriate as part of the advocate's armoury. Try to express yourself in elegant language, in 'Courtly English'. One of the worst advocates I have ever seen was addressing the court (in a light suit) in a matrimonial case and he said: 'And the thing that gets up my nose, Your Worship, is that there are young children here, and I'm a father myself.' His Worship was Sir Frank Milton, a former Chief Metropolitan Magistrate, who commented: 'The state of your nasal organ is not of the slightest interest to me. Kindly do not introduce such an irrelevant protuberance again.'

Do not dwell on the obvious in your closing speeches, and do credit an experienced Bench with a modicum of knowledge and common sense. Magistrates, lay and stipendiary, do not welcome being harangued on the burden of proof, although there is nothing wrong in alluding briefly to it at the end of your closing speech in some such form as: 'In the light of the many discrepancies in the prosecution case to which I have endeavoured to draw your attention, could you ever be sure, as the law requires you to be, of the defendant's guilt in this case?'

The judge sitting alone, and lay and stipendiary magistrates too, will sometimes welcome the use of attractive figurative language even when you are enumerating your main points as I suggested earlier. I once had to defend a tenant against whom possession was claimed under five (I think all five) of the then Rent Act headings. I began my closing address thus:

'May it please your Honour, in this case five fingers are

stretching out to grasp possession of his home from this unhappy man.' I then went on to seek to show how none of the five heads of claim had been made out, and I finished my speech with these words: 'Your Honour, in my submission each one of those greedy, grasping fingers has been broken, and the defendant is entitled to live on in the peace and tranquillity of his home'. I have to admit that the county court judge did not agree with me, and found against me under all five heads, but I thought it was worth trying!

In that case I tried to copy a dramatist for whom I have great admiration, Arthur Wing Pinero, the architect of 'the well-made play'. In his dramas, which usually observe the classical unities of time, place and action (not so easy to control in the forensic setting!) he frequently reminds the audience, often ironically, at the end of the play, of how it all began. I think that it is good to link the end of your speech with the beginning, reminding the court that there was a beginning—not, one hopes, too long ago.

In the second chapter I referred to my first appearance in the Court of Appeal and my first appearance in the Court of Criminal Appeal. I would like now to write about the first jury trial in which I ever took part. It was noteworthy for three reasons: my opponent was Edward Clarke, and one of the members of the jury was the late Terence Rattigan, the playwright. (I fully expected that he would write a modern version of *The Winslow Boy* after listening to my forensic efforts, but I regret to say that he did not, although he was kind enough to write a letter to me afterwards.) The judge was Frank Cassels, surely one of the most delightful judges before whom one could hope to appear in one's early (or any) days.

The defendant was an ex-Royal Navy Petty Officer of impeccable character (and I too am an ex-Royal Navy Petty Officer, with no previous convictions) who faced four separate charges of stealing groceries from the store of which he had become manager following his honourable discharge from the Royal Navy. I can quote verbatim the beginning and ending of my closing speech, because I wrote it all out in full, and I still possess it (not a practice that I now advocate). It began as follows:

'May it please your Lordship, members of the jury, this man, who has served his country faithfully and well for twenty-five years in the Royal Navy, often in times of great danger, now finds that he has sailed into a kind of dock with which he is wholly unfamiliar . . .'

'Some time later', I concluded my address as follows: 'Members of the jury, this man has served his country faithfully and well, often in times of peril. All that he now asks is that his fellow countrymen should serve him by the like token—faithfully and well.'

I say 'some time later'—I hope not too much later. Always remember that you do not make a speech eternal by making it everlasting. The best advice that I ever heard as to the proper length of a speech came from the late Recorder of Cambridge, Sir Roland Burrows KC who said: 'A speech should be like a lady's dress: short enough to be interesting, but long enough to cover the subject matter'.

7 Your witness: the technique of examination-in-chief and re-examination

Many books have been written on the art of cross-examination, mostly by American attorneys keen to advertise their own expertise in this sphere. I may be wrong, but so far as I know this is the first article ever to be written specifically about the less exciting topics of examination-in-chief and re-examination.

The eliciting of evidence takes place mainly through the questioning of witnesses, and this is effected in three stages—examination-in-chief, cross-examination and re-examination. Stages 1 and 3 take place with your own witness and basically the same rules apply to these two stages. Cross-examination is the questioning of witnesses on the other side, and to these witnesses you are allowed to put leading questions. That of course leads to the question: What is a leading question? A leading question is a question which suggests or tends to suggest to the witness the answer which he should give. Such questions can never be asked in re-examination, and may only be asked of one's own client or witnesses on matters not in issue in the case, such as the witness's name, occupation, and address—though not even his address in some cases in the Family Division where domicile may be in issue. One of my colleagues at the Bar got weary of a judge in that division who was constantly accusing him of leading, and put this question to a minor witness: 'Who are you?'

May I give examples of non-leading and leading questions? An action is being brought against the committee of a social club and it is desired to prove that there is too much familiarity at the dances that they organise. It is not open to the advocate for the complainants to ask: 'Is it true that the members dance cheek to cheek at these functions?' The question would have to be put in some neutral and colourless form, such as: 'Could you give his Lordship some idea of the approximate distance between the various partners during the terpsichore?'

On the other hand, supposing that the answer to the non-leading question just posed satisfied the advocate for the complainants, it would be open to the advocate appearing for the committee of the social club to put a leading question in cross-examination. He would be quite entitled to ask:

'It is true, isn't it, that when you have 200 couples dancing together in a small room it is a physical impossibility for them to do so at a distance of less than 18 inches from each other?'

Of all the legal subjects to be learned by the would-be advocate, evidence is by far the most important, and should be the subject of constant study, because the advocate who allows his opponent to slip in the inadmissible question resulting in the inadmissible answer may lose his case thereby—(especially before a Bench of lay justices)—while the advocate who keeps objecting when there is nothing to object to tries the patience of the Bench and his opponent and gets the general reputation of being very objectionable.

Examination-in-chief is an underrated, neglected art. Yet the most convincing story is the one that is elicited smoothly and easily, by the advocate and the witness. A concert is enjoyable only if the conductor and the orchestra are working in harmony; a car journey is satisfying only if both the car and the driver are operating in unison. The advocate is the conductor or driver, the witness is the orchestra or car, victory is the prize, the end of the journey, or the coda. To make the journey through the case run smoothly the advocate should have had a rehearsal or practice run together with his client in Chambers or his office or at least outside the court. It is often very difficult to get the answers you want without leading.

I well remember one Saturday afternoon at Lambeth Magistrates' Court when counsel was trying to get the complainant to say that the respondent had struck him in the stomach during a fight. The only reason I know this is because I was in the next case but one, and I slipped out to ask counsel what he had wanted his client to say— after the case had been dismissed. (I used to do a lot of assault cases at Lambeth on Saturday afternoons: I had a very high class practice in my early days!) It went like this:

'What did he do?' asked counsel.

'Well, he hit me', replied the complainant.

'Where did he hit you?'

'In the street sir.'

'No, no, on what part of your anatomy?' Now that was a bad question. The driver and the car were not in the same gear. The witness became suspicious. He did not know up to then that he had an anatomy, and he did not like being accused of having one by his lawyer, so he decided to change direction.

'Well, he kicked me.'

'Ah, where did he kick you?'

'Just at the entrance.'

'At the entrance to what?' counsel asked, rather apprensively.

'The entrance to my flat, sir.'

Counsel then gave up, with a despairing gesture. What a bad thing it is to make despairing gestures, like the turning of palms upwards, the rolling of eyes heavenwards, the throwing of papers downwards, showing that you do not believe in your client! If you don't, why on earth should the Bench?

'I don't suppose you want to cross-examine' the stipendiary magistrate murmured, wearily. Counsel on the other side wisely took the hint. Some wouldn't, but he got the message, and the complainant's counsel (who to his credit, had asked no leading questions) then called the complainant's wife. She was an eager, bustling little woman who started to give her evidence almost before she got into the witness-box.

'I saw him strike my husband', she volunteered helpfully.

'And where did he strike him?'

'On the path outside.'

All this fiasco could have been avoided by a careful rehearsal beforehand. It clearly had not taken place.

In 1955 I was invigilating in the Bar Examinations for the Council of Legal Education. Suddenly a worried member of their staff rushed up to me and said: 'You're on, in PDA 5 now. I'll take over.' (It was one of many occasions on which my clerk of those days 'missed a case' in the list. 'It's just one of those things, sir', he used to explain. A worse disaster was to befall me when he missed one in the Court of Appeal. What a relief it was to move some years later to a set where the clerks were really efficient! The young barrister would be well advised to examine his potential clerk carefully before applying to join a set of Chambers.) Anyway, I rushed down to the Divorce Court, apologised to the judge (the late Willmer J) for being late—he was charming in his celebrated gruff way—and I started to open a case which I had not looked at for about a year—since I had settled the petition. To my horror I realised that it was a case with a lot of law in it. Indeed it was to become a leading authority on the possibility of desertion when the parties were living under the same roof. (An eminent divorce practitioner told me afterwards that I had persuaded the judge to make one of the worst decisions ever pronounced in matrimonial law!) At all events, I decided that if I could keep the case going all day, that would enable me to look up the law overnight and to make my closing speech, supported by numerous authorities, the next day.

But a more immediate problem was to present itself. The petitioner, Mr Fishburn, was the vaguest man I have ever met. Desertion in those days had to be for a continuous period of at least three years. According to the particulars of desertion in the petition which I had settled in 1954 the wife had moved into her own part of the matrimonial home in 1949, since when she had never spoken to her husband or done anything for him. I got Mr Fishburn to say that his wife had moved out, but the question was, when? 'I think it was about a year ago', said Mr Fishburn, unhelpfully. 'Well, that won't do', said the judge firmly, preparing to dismiss the case there and then.

'Which year was it?' I asked, hopefully.

'1937', he replied.

'Was it before or after the war?' I enquired in bewilderment.

'It depends which war you mean', said Mr Fishburn, belligerently.

Eventually, I thought of the ploy of asking my rather forgetful client if he could remember any event that had occurred since World War Two. He recalled the Festival of Britain (which took place in the autumn of 1951).

'Did she leave you before or after the Festival of Britain?' I enquired, desperately. Mr Fishburn was contrary by nature. 'Neither before nor after', he replied, 'It was during the Festival of Britain.' I had got that far without any too objectionable leading questions.

Happily, the festival had finished about three years and one week before I had settled the petition, and the generous judge, who had watched my struggles with obvious amusement, kindly agreed to my application to amend the date of desertion in the petition and the evidence-in-chief proceeded on its rather dreary way.

It was to be enlivened greatly, however, when my opponent, now the Recorder of London, rose to cross-examine. His simple, direct question was the most effective first question in cross-examination that I have ever heard.

'Mr Fishburn', he asked. 'Do you love your wife?'

'What, a woman like that!' exclaimed Mr Fishburn. 'I hate her like poison.' To obtain a divorce on the ground of desertion in those days the petitioner had to show that he was willing to resume cohabitation with the errant spouse. Both sides were refused a decree. I doubt though if they are still married (or even alive). I think that union 'broke down irretrievably' long ago. (So did my association with my instructing solicitor!)

That was a case in which I had no opportunity of a conference with the lay client before the case. In another case where I had such a conference (advisable whenever possible) it did no good to me or to my lay client. It was an affiliation case. The complainant was a charming 'peaches and cream' Cockney girl of some seventeen summers (and no more than eighteen winters) who was alleging that a certain young man whom she had known for a long time was the father of her child.

'Tell me', I said in conference, 'have you ever been intimate with any other young men?' (I asked the question shyly, fully expecting an indignant negative response. I was young and very ingenuous in those days!)

'Oh yers', she replied.

'Really', I exclaimed in astonishment. 'How many?'

She counted on the fingers of both hands. 'Seven', she decided, eventually.

'Tell me about them', I said, unhappily, and she gave me names and addresses, and all the details. But it seemed from the dates of the affairs that none of them could possibly be the father of her child, so I said: 'Well, I'm sure your present young man must know about all these others, and I think it will be best if I ask you about all these earlier affairs when I am questioning you in court, rather than leaving them to be dragged from you in cross-examination by the defending advocate. Don't you agree?'

'Well, you're the barrister', she commented, pragmatically.

'Yes, I am', I said firmly, 'and that's the way we're going to do it.'

(I still think, despite the disaster that was to follow, that I was right in my tactics. If the advocate is sure that the other side is going to cross-examine on some point to his client's discredit, it is best to deal with it in chief. The client's advocate can bring the matter out in a light much less embarrassing to him, and indeed the client gains kudos or merit in the eyes of the court for his initial frankness.)

We appeared in my affiliation case, nearly forty years ago, before Sybil Campbell, the only lady London stipendiary. She looked like everybody's auntie, but was the terror of the dockers, because she did not understand the doctrine of 'perks'. On the other hand I always felt that if I were accused of an offence of which I was not guilty I would as soon be tried by her as by a jury—and you can't pay a higher compliment to a magistrate than that. She was not however very sympathetic to young unmarried girls who had babies. I adopted the tactics I had discussed with the girl in conference, but I could see the magistrate's face getting longer as the list of intimate acquaintances got longer, so when I had asked about the last one I passed quickly to something else.

'Just a moment, Mr Crowther', interrupted the magistrate. 'I wish to ask this gal [all young ladies were "gals" in her court] a question. Tell me, my gal, have you ever been intimate with any other men, apart from those just mentioned?'

'Nah, I don't think so', replied the 'gal' casually.

'You don't think so: aren't you sure?' asked the magistrate.

'Well', said the complainant reflectively, 'there's always Spud Baker.'

'Spud Baker', mouthed the magistrate with displeasure. 'Then why did you not mention this—er—Mr Baker when your counsel was going through what I can only describe as this catalogue?' (I could tell that things were not going very well for us by now.)

'Oh well', replied the witness disarmingly, 'old Spud—'e don't count. All the girls round 'ere 'ave been intimate with Spud Baker.'

The magistrate decided that the time had come for the exercise of a little judicial irony (usually a mistake, as I can confirm from the occasions when I have tried to exercise it). She drew herself up to her full height: '*I* have never been intimate with Spud Baker', she said with dignity and conviction.

The Cockney girl's response was quick and effective. 'No, I don't suppose you 'ave', she said. 'It's only the young and pretty ones old Spud goes after.'

I lost that case, but I started to learn to live with life, an essential element in the career of the lawyer.

If a witness appears not to have heard a question it may be *not* that he is deaf in the accepted meaning of the term, and so needing to have the question repeated 20 decibels louder, but that he is mentally deaf—not understanding too quickly in the unfamiliar surroundings of the courtroom. So, when you ask the question again, put it in a different, simpler form. 'I'm sorry, I mean, on what part of your body?' counsel should have asked, in the 'anatomy' case I referred to earlier. Don't get impatient or angry, or your client will feel that even the person he most expects to be on his side is turning against him. And it sometimes helps if you can couch the question in some homely phrase such as: 'Would you care to tell the magistrates what happened next?' I never had a client so surly as to reply, 'No, I wouldn't'.

Get your client well positioned. It's the most natural thing in the world to turn towards the person who is questioning you, yet this will help to make your witness inaudible to the Bench. If your witness cannot be persuaded to face the magistrates, try this lotion on him: 'Now, turn your ear towards me and you will hear what I am saying. Turn your mouth towards the magistrates and they will hear what you are saying.'

Also, beforehand, take out an insurance policy on the witness who is going to say too much. The worst offenders in this respect tend to be nervous middle-aged women who declare: 'O—oh, I'm so worried, when I get in there I shan't be able to say a word' but once they 'get their head' they are like Tennyson's Brook. Take control before you get into court. 'Give short answers to my questions. If you don't say enough, I can always ask you another question, but if you say too much. I won't be able to stop you.' The good sense of this advice occasionally seeps through.

And, for your part, make sure that all your questions are short, crisp, direct and uncomplicated. Don't engage in convoluted questions with lots of subordinate clauses—they will not be understood by either the witness or the court. Even a short question can be unduly complex. 'Did you enjoy kissing the Respondent under the mistletoe on Christmas Eve?' is in fact four questions. The questioning should go: 'Did you kiss the Respondent?' 'Where did it happen?' 'When?' 'Did you enjoy it?'; because if you put it in the first form an experienced witness would be quite entitled to score off you by asking: 'Which of those questions would you like me to answer first?'

If in a criminal case your client has a good character, for heaven's sake put it in, as early as possible. Cross-examine the police officer in charge of the case about it, and get your client to reiterate it in chief. I never cease to be amazed how many advocates fail to do this. Often your client's good character, even in a motoring case, is one of the greatest assets you have. 'Good name in man or woman, good my Lord, is the immediate jewel of our souls.' Why neglect to make it sparkle? But make sure you check with the prosecution first. Sometimes your client won't want you to know of his twelve previous convictions: it might cause you to lose confidence in him, and you will have a nasty shock when you start asking about the sterling quality of his integrity. Approach the officer in charge of the case (with the permission of the prosecuting advocate) before the case begins, to establish his attitude. Then you will avoid this sort of disaster which I once observed at the Old Bailey:

Counsel: 'The defendant is a man of impeccable character, is he not, Inspector?'

The Inspector (grudgingly, looking at a file): 'Well, he's never been convicted, if that's what you mean'.

Counsel: 'Why are you being so ungenerous, officer?'

Inspector: 'Because I don't like a man who's been acquitted three times of armed robbery on false alibis'.

If your client has got a bad character, and the other side does not know, you are under no obligation to reveal it. If the policeman says 'nothing known' you do not have to get up and say, 'Oh yes, there is, he is subject to a suspended sentence'. Lord Goddard is the authority for this. Whatever anyone may say about Lord Goddard, he was a practical man of commonsense. His reasoning was that no defendant would reveal his previous record in such circumstances. Why should a person be worse off because he was paying for the services of solicitor and/or counsel (as most defendants did in his day)? But you must not go on and make capital out of the situation. You must not, in mitigation, say: 'As you have heard he has no convictions', or 'He is of course a man of excellent character'—that would be deliberately dishonest, and your first priority must be to be honest with the court, so just leave well alone. This is consonant with the ruling given by the Law Society following the *Bridgwood* case in 1988, for a fuller account of which see p 137.

The same rules apply to re-examination as to examination-in-chief, except that re-examination is strictly limited to matters arising out of cross-examination, and as it is always concerned with matters seriously in issue, you must never, never lead in re-examination. A solicitor who, when I, as counsel appearing against him, complained bitterly of his leading, replied: 'But this is re-examination', showed great ignorance of the law of evidence.

Re-examination is an over-rated, over-exposed part of the advocate's job. It is a rescue operation, designed to restore some semblance of order to the havoc created by the cross-examination. If you rise to re-examine, you are thereby impliedly admitting that damage has been done to your case in cross-examination. If you do not think that any serious damage has been done, just say 'No re-examination, thank you'. (This is much to be preferred to: 'I have no need to re-examine this witness', which sounds both pompous and complacent.) This is not to say that re-examination is not sometimes necessary, especially with an honest witness who has got confused, or if you think the Bench may have got confused, but there are many cases in which it does more harm than good. Never try to slip in new matter under the guise of re-examination. If you forgot to put an important question in chief and have remembered it during the cross-examination, ask the court's leave to put it after re-examining; they will always grant it, subject of course to your opponent's right to cross-examination on that matter—and on that matter alone.

As I have mentioned before, for many years I gave free advice at Toynbee Hall Legal Advice Centre. The Centre has been in existence for over a hundred years and I advised there for longer than any other lawyer except for John Clark, one of the best lawyers I have ever known, now the Secretary of the National Association of Parish Councils. I strongly advise all young lawyers to follow John's and my example, either at Toynbee, or some other Legal Advice Centre. My motives were not entirely altruistic. As a barrister, I wanted to learn something of the solicitor's job. When taking statements from 'clients' I operated the discipline of never asking a leading question: this, I thought, would assist me in examination-in-chief and re-examination. Whether it did or not I cannot be sure, but I do know that it made me much more understanding of the difficulties of solicitors who sent me briefs containing incoherent or incomprehensible witness statements!

8 Your witness: the business of cross-examination

There have been several books on 'The Art of Cross-Examination' and 'The Technique of Cross-Examination', but cross-examination is not always an art or a technical operation; however, it should, at the very least, be carried out in a business-like fashion; hence my rather prosaic title to this chapter.

Every business has its rules. The first rule of cross-examination is that the defence (whether the case be criminal or civil) must be put to the plaintiff's or prosecution witnesses in cross-examination. Evidence cannot be called to contradict matters not challenged in cross-examination. It is up to the advocate to decide through which witness he will make his challenge—challenges do not necessarily get stronger through being made many times over or even more than once—but certainly all matters that are in dispute must be made plain during the plaintiff's or the prosecution case.

I once witnessed the following distressing scene in the old Balham Magistrates' Court. A wife was seeking a separation order on the grounds of persistent cruelty. When she had completed her evidence the young barrister defending said: 'No questions'. Likewise he had 'no questions' for each of her witnesses. When the complainant's case was complete, the barrister said: 'I will now call my client'. 'You will do no such thing', said Glen Craske, the stipendiary magistrate, fiercely, 'You have challenged none of the evidence called on behalf of the complainant, which I am therefore entitled to accept as being true. I find this case proved.' Craske had the reputation of being a good lawyer, but a bad magistrate. What he did was perfectly correct in law, but had little to do with justice.

So PUT YOUR CASE in cross-examination, and put it early on. Remember that up to the moment when you rise to cross-examine, the justices or the jury have not heard a word in favour of your client. It is therefore very important to make an impact with your first question. If possible let it go right to the heart of the matter, like Sir James Miskin's first question in *Fishburn* v *Fishburn* (referred to in the last chapter): 'Do you love your wife?' Give a lot of thought to that first question. All the rest of your cross-examination should derive from it. In cross-examination as in all advocacy, always have a plan, a pattern, and a purpose. Every question must have an aim in view. Always be ready for that devastating intervention from the Bench: 'To what issue in this case is that question directed?'

With experience, all good advocates develop their own special styles of cross-examination. I have never had the pleasure of meeting or appearing before Mrs Justice Heilbron, so I hope that what I am about to say of her—based entirely on hearsay evidence—is accurate. As Rose Heilbron QC, she was one of the greatest advocates in the North of England. One who knew her well said that her practice was to draw a chart for her cross-examination: if the witness answers 'Yes' to my first question I will proceed along this line, and if 'No' I will go in this direction; so that her overnight notes looked like a genealogical tree. Thus she would be prepared for anything.

Norman Birkett, whose name was a household word fifty years ago, would take his time as, like a conscientious spider, he courteously wove a web of apparently innocuous questions around his hapless victim, before suddenly plunging with deadly precision to the heart of the matter. I remember Sir Norman well; his great adversary in so many famous cases, Sir Patrick Hastings, not so well. He was a very different sort of advocate, a man of few words. I once heard him on the radio, on a programme called 'The Brains' Trust'. 'What is the difference', asked a questioner, 'between libel and slander?' 'Libel is written, slander spoken', replied Sir Patrick. This not completely adequate response constituted the longest answer that he gave during the whole programme! He is said to have written an opinion consisting of one word: 'Yes'—and to have charged 1,000 guineas for it!

Norman Birkett in his capacity as Chairman of the Government Committee appointed to advise on wartime internment had to question Sir Oswald Mosley, founder of the British Union of Fascists. The interrogation which began on 2 July 1940, lasted sixteen hours, and part of it is now available for scrutiny due to the release of the official papers by the Public Record Office. It makes fascinating reading, as we observe one brilliant mind pitted against another.

Birkett: 'Part of the policy of the British Union is to stop all immigration, is it not?'

Mosley: 'Stop all foreigners coming in, but gradually and humanely to get rid of all foreigners who are here'.

Birkett: 'That is to say, this country would no longer be, as it was in the old days, an asylum for the oppresed?'

Mosley: 'Oh, certainly'.

It is interesting to see how far, in recent times, official policy has veered away from Birkett's concept of this country being 'as it was in the old days, an asylum for the oppressed' towards Sir Oswald's less generous attitude.

Mosley remained active politically almost until his death. In the early 1960s I had the task of defending one of his henchmen. My telephone at home rang the evening before the trial and I answered it. A clear and powerful voice addressed me.

'This is Sir Oswald Mosley speaking from Paris. You are defending one of my men tomorrow. I want to discuss tactics.'

It gave me great pleasure to say that the rules of my profession allowed me to discuss the case only with my instructing solicitor and the uneducated, inarticulate lay client. There is a lot of benefit to be derived from keeping the two branches of the legal profession separate which I hope Parliament will bear in mind as it considers the Courts and Legal Services Bill. It would have been difficult for a solicitor to have rebuffed him.

Hastings had a rule (which he did not actually observe in the *Laski* libel case) that he aimed to ask not more than three questions of the main witness on the other side. But what devastating questions they were, devised with such cunning preparation!

At a fairly early stage of my career at the Bar I decided that Sir Patrick's style was not mine. However, I did apply this 'three questions' rule whenever I was prosecuting in careless driving cases. And if I thought that I needed to ask more than three questions of the defendant driver, I usually felt that the case deserved to be lost. In many instances one can crystallise the whole of the prosecution's case of careless driving into just one question such as: 'Could this accident possibly have occurred if you had been keeping a proper look-out?' (or 'if you had been driving at a safe distance from the car in front?') This technique is greatly to be preferred to that of one prosecutor who frequently appeared before me in this type of case. I have known him to cross-examine the defendant for over an hour, the witness appearing firmer and more reliable in his recollection as he gained in confidence through becoming familiar with his position in the witness-box. This advocate also had the habit of appearing to have finished cross-examining when he had not done so, by half sitting down. On one occasion when he got into his crouching position I asked: 'Any re-examination?' of his opponent, and the prosecutor was so surprised that he slumped into his seat. He quickly rose again to protest: 'But I haven't finished yet'. 'Oh yes, you have', I said. 'Next witness please'.

Sir Patrick Hastings may not have been very generous with words, but he was effusive in his praise of his old rival after the latter's spectacular success in the *Mancini* case. This is what Sir Patrick said: 'If it should ever be my lot to cut up a lady and put her body in an unwanted suitcase, I should unhesitatingly place my future in Norman Birkett's hands. He would convince the jury that (a) I was not there; (b) I had not cut up the lady and (c) If I had done so, she thoroughly deserved it.'

Another great cross-examiner with a different style was the ironical Sir Edward Carson, to whose brilliance in cross-examination the witty Oscar Wilde in large measure owed his downfall and his degradation. In one case Sir Edward was cross-examining a truculent witnes with a very red nose.

'Do you drink?' asked Sir Edward.

'That's my business', snapped the witness.

'Any other?' asked Sir Edward.

It is very important to remember, as Richard Du Cann has said, that cross-examination does not mean examining crossly. In civil cases the advocate usually stands near his witnesses when they are giving evidence, but questions the witnesses on the other side *across* the court. There is no excuse for rudeness in cross-examination—no excuse ever for rudeness in court. The most deadly cross-examiners that I have ever seen, including Norman Birkett, Sebag Shaw, Victor Durand, John Hazan and Jeremy Hutchinson, have been the most courteous. They could afford to be patient. They knew exactly where they were going. They had prepared their cross-examinations well.

In the sensational murder case brought against Dr Bodkin Adams in 1957, two of the doctor's nurses gave evidence against him of his hastening on their way to a better world wealthy patients who had made wills in the solicitous doctor's favour. The nurses were having to recall events of many years earlier—matters of which they had not then complained—never an easy task. One of them gave part of her evidence on one day, but was warned by the trial judge, Devlin J not to talk about the case to any other witness.

The case centred on Eastbourne, where the doctor had had his practice, but most of the witnesses came from Brighton. Defending counsel, Geoffrey Lawrence QC rightly surmised that in those days when the train service between London and Brighton was quick, reliable and relatively cheap, both girls might travel down to Brighton that evening on the same train—even in the same carriage—returning to London early next day. It was arranged that there should be another passenger in the same carriage, making a note. His duties began when the second nurse, who had yet to give evidence, looked up from her evening paper to remark to the first girl words to the effect: 'You didn't say that, did you? It's not right'. You can imagine what a field day Geoffrey Lawrence had with the two nurses with the conversation that ensued between them after that. And it enabled him slyly to include in his closing speech that telling sentence to which I referred in an earlier chapter:

> 'What you read in the papers, what you hear in the train, what you hear in the cafés and the restaurants, what your friends and relations come and tell you, rumour, gossip, all the rest of it, may be so wrong.'

But none of this would have been possible without the most intelligent anticipation, the most careful preparation. Lazy by nature, I have to convey to you the sad news that there is no substitute for hard work in advocacy. When the great trial was over, and when Dr Adams had been acquitted without being called to give evidence, the diarist of *The Times* commented on how throughout that long and arduous trial Geoffrey Lawrence had never once lost his temper, shown impatience, or even raised his voice. Soon afterwards he was made a High Court judge. It was a tragedy that he was to die within weeks of his appointment. Dr Adams, on the other hand, lived on for more than a quarter of a century, and Lord Devlin's book about the trial, called *Easing the Passing*, makes compelling reading.

Courtesy is not only an admirable quality; it is essential both on the Bench itself and in the advocates' benches. I remember only one occasion at the Bar on which I allowed my natural indignation to get the better of me. A very prim and proper looking middle-aged man had recently acquired a property in which the sitting tenant, a rather dirty but really quite sweet old boy of eighty-two, had been living for most of his life, and the landlord sought possession on the only ground open to him, viz nuisance and annoyance, one of the allegations of nuisance being of assault. My first question in cross-examination, designed to call attention to the ridiculousness of the allegation, was: 'Were you very frightened when this old man assaulted you?' In advocacy, as in real life, reserve bullying for the bully, and, fortunately one does not meet many bullies in the witness-box (although we have all come across the occasional bullying judge, and it is the advocate's duty to stand up courageously—yet courteously—to him).

I remember with particular satisfaction a quiet cross-examination of a sweet-looking but, alas, untruthful young woman, which culminated in a Scottish judge murmuring quietly to her: 'You know, it's sad to see someone so young and so attractive telling such lies'. That was achieved with no shouting, no fuss.

Preparation involves a close study of all the documents in the case, being utterly familiar with them, however long it may take, however boring it may seem. A witness will often have forgotten what he wrote months or years earlier and there is no more effective cross-examination than to put to him a contemporaneous document contradicting the evidence he is giving now.

I just used the expression 'to put to him'. Cross-examination is not enhanced by the use of such expressions as 'I must put it to you', or 'My instructions are . . .' or, worst of all, 'the defendant and his witnesses will go into the witness box and will take the oath and say . . .' Avoid all this verbiage, which only gives the witness time to think up what may be untruthful answers. Keep up the pressure with questions that are short (five or six words if possible), brisk, and to the point. A good cross-examination sounds like machine-gun fire, and is often equally deadly.

When the unexpected witness is called, ask him the unexpected question, ie the question which *he* is not expecting. When agreeing in the magistrates' court to a committal under s 6(2) of the Magistrates' Courts Act 1980, consider carefully what witnesses you want called at the trial, what witnesses you are prepared to have conditionally bound. I once watched Lord Justice Lawton, as a junior barrister, cross-examine a plan drawer at some length in a case of dangerous (now reckless) driving before a jury. One can learn a lot from watching a really good advocate at work, and I put the lesson learned that day to good effect a little later. My client also appeared before a jury, charged with dangerous driving. The allegation against him was simply that he had driven around the bend of a steep hill in Mill Hill, North London, at 45 mph (it being a 30 mph area). I went to have a view—always a wise thing to do if possible, especially in motoring cases. The hill was steep, but the bend was a very slight one. Its degree was not clear from the plan, so I decided to have the plan drawer called. I put to him the following questions, and elicited the following answers:

Q There appears to be a bend on the plan. Would you agree with me that it is a very slight bend?
A Yes.
Q Almost imperceptible really?
A Yes.

He was an honest witness, with no axe to grind. When the first of the two traffic officers who had stopped the defendant gave evidence, I asked these questions:

Q Why, if he was merely going at 45 mph, did you not simply charge him with speeding?
A Because of the bend, sir.
Q The bend made all the difference between a trivial charge and a really serious one?
A Yes, sir.
Q Would you then describe that bend to the jury?
A Well, it's a really sharp bend, and very dangerous to go round it at 45 mph, because you might not see traffic coming the other way and you could easily lose control and cause a collision.

The poor policeman could not understand why the jury started to shake with mirth, and I doubt if he ever realised why the case got 'laughed out of court'.

In an earlier chapter I mentioned that your client's good character (if he has one) in a criminal case may be your (and his) greatest asset. If you are sure about it—and you can be sure only after checking with the prosecution, because there are defendants who do not even tell the truth to their lawyers—get it in early, by cross-examining the first police officer about it: 'The defendant is a man of impeccable character, is he not?' or 'It is true, is it not, that the defendant has no previous convictions?' (whichever you deem the more appropriate) and then reinforce this by asking the defendant in chief about his good record. If you attack the character of the prosecution witnesses or if you suggest that the police have conspired together to make a false case against your client, eg by planting a knife or drugs or stolen property upon him, you let in your client's bad character *provided that he goes into the witness box to give evidence*—see *R* v *Butterwasser* (1948) 111 JP 527.

If he maintains his 'right of silence', his previous convictions cannot be introduced. But before you start suggesting to witnesses for the prosecution that they have previous convictions, make sure that you have the memoranda of their convictions, or their Criminal Records Office forms, in your hand. The prosecution are under a duty to give these documents to you, and even to inform you of convictions of prosecution witnesses of which you may be unaware, so as to enable you to make your own judgment on this important issue. In my days at the Bar this was the practice of prosecutors everywhere throughout the country except in Essex—but I believe that there has been a change of heart even in Essex now.

Only once in my time at the Bar, and that in my very early days, did I go to the West Ham Magistrates' Court, and, as a result of my experience that day, I was glad that I was never to be sent there again. The court was presided over by a very old stipendiary magistrate called JP Eddy, and when he eventually retired (to take up the occupation of writing almost daily to *The Times*) I could quite understand why it was decided to replace him by a lay Bench.

The case was both sad and dramatic. The defendant,

whom I was briefed to represent, was a carpenter of previous good character accused of an assault occasioning actual bodily harm upon his wife's lover. His defence was that his wife had left him and the children to go to live with the lover, that he was naturally distressed by this, and, on his way home from work on the day following her desertion of him, he had called at the lover's address to plead with the wife to return. The lover had produced a knife, and gone to attack the defendant with it, whereupon the defendant had remembered his hammer which he had with him in his tool kit, and injured the complainant with it in reasonable self-defence. When I arrived at the court I was greeted by the court gaoler in this way: 'Oh, you're defending, are you sir? I'm glad about that. We don't like the complainant in this case. He's a very violent man. He's got a long string of previous. He's been done twice at the Old Bailey—once for assault on police when he got three years and once for unlawful wounding when he got five. I wish you well, sir. Your client seems a nice chap.'

But a little later the same gaoler said to me: 'I think I've told you too much, sir. Use the information in any way you like, but please don't reveal where you got it from.'

So, in due course, I rose to cross-examine the complainant. 'You yourself are no stranger to violence, are you?' I asked him.

'What do you mean?'

'You have been sentenced to three years for assault on police and five years for unlawful wounding'.

'No I haven't.'

'Will you show the complainant the memoranda of convictions?' demanded the magistrate.

'I'm afraid I do not have them', I replied.

'Then on what do you base these serious allegations?'

'On information from a source that I believe to be reliable', I replied.

'Then reveal your source'.

'I'm afraid that I am not in a position to do so.'

'No, you are not in a position to do so because you are making it all up. These are most disgraceful allegations against a perfectly respectable man, and I shall consider reporting you to your Benchers.'

He did not do so, but I afterwards established that the allegations that I was making were true. The prosecution did not try to help me out of my dilemma, although they must have had details of the complainant's previous convictions—but then, West Ham is almost in Essex. But I learned a salutary lesson that day: never suggest to a witness that he has been guilty of a crime (even if he has) unless you hold the record of that crime in your hand.

There are three other pieces of advice about cross-examination that very senior advocates will always give to novices, so I will pass them on, although I do not entirely agree with the first two of them.

'Never cross-examine a witness who has done you no harm.' This admonition should be qualified, I think, by the advice of considering putting to the unexpected witness the question that he is not expecting. Who could be a more 'harmless' witness than the plan drawers in the two cases (of Lawton LJ and myself) that I mentioned earlier in this chapter? Yet each was cross-examined to some effect.

'Never ask a question to which you do not know the answer.' This is one of the pieces of advice most frequently given to young advocates and I do not agree with it. Certainly one must not flounder on fishing expeditions in cross-examination, but if the primary task of the court is to get at the truth of the matter and the most important duty of the advocate is to assist the court in ensuring that justice be done, how can the advocate leave certain matters of which he is unaware in an area of darkness? Lay justices, in particular, seem afraid to ask questions—in case they ask the wrong ones—and it is surely the duty of the advocates on both sides to illuminate the obscure areas of the case.

This rule, if strictly observed, would deter the advocate from asking the 'inspired' question, based on intelligent intuition, which can change the whole complexion of a case.

I have referred a lot in this book to the Dr Adams murder case. The 'Rainbow Murder' had little in common with it, except that both cases were transferred from provincial towns to be tried at the Old Bailey because local feeling in each case was so strong that prejudice in local juries was feared, and Edward Clarke appeared in both cases. There the similarities ended. The trial of Bodkin Adams was widely reported in the national press for several weeks; the 'Rainbow Murder' earned a few columns in the *East Suffolk Gazette* one evening.

A very distinguished silk, about to become a High Court judge, led for the defence of Dr Adams. I represented one of the defendants in the *Rainbow* case.

The *Rainbow* was a rather seedy public house in Ipswich. In 1960 an Irish barman there refused to serve four West Indians with drink. They reacted strongly to the insult. One of them went outside and threw a brick through the window and, in the ensuing chaos, the barman was stabbed twice in the back, with two different knives, and he died. All four West Indians were charged with murder. Strangely enough, the one who was outside the public house at the time of the stabbing, throwing a brick through the window, was convicted by the jury—presumably on the rather Machiavellian view that he had started all the trouble—but he got off on appeal. As against one of the other West Indians the evidence was overwhelming—he was asked only two questions in the witness box:

Counsel for the defence: 'Did you murder Mr O'Brien?'

Defendant: 'No'.

Counsel for the prosecution: 'But you killed him, didn't you?'

Defendant: 'Yes'.

He was convicted.

That left two more defendants, one more knife, one more stab wound. Which of them had inflicted it?

For reasons never quite clear to me the trial judge, Thesiger J, always referred to the defendant I represented, a local taxi driver, as 'Terry Thomas'. Thomas was his surname, but Terry was not his Christian name. However, I would not like to differ from a High Court judge, so I will call him 'Terry Thomas'.

He was bumptious and arrogant, but also extremely

intelligent; so much so that I felt constrained to say this to him in conference: 'I know that you are highly intelligent, and I also know that you know that you are highly intelligent. You may find that you are more intelligent than prosecuting counsel. Please don't try to score off him in court. The jury won't like it if you do.' He was clever enough to follow that advice, and appeared subdued and polite in court, without a sign of arrogance, intellectual or physical. Even Mr Justice Thesiger seemed to like 'Terry Thomas'.

There were over 30 prosecution witnesses. 'The *Rainbow* was a popular establishment. Committals were all 'old style' then, and the proceedings in the magistrates' court lasted three days. Most of the witnesses for the prosecution lacked sophistication and charm (The chairman of the lay Bench remarked afterwards that he had never seen a more unattractive parade of human flesh.) Most of the witnesses put Terry Thomas well away from the immediate vicinity of the barman at the material time. Things were going well for him throughout most of the committal. Then a witness was called who changed everything. She was a statuesque blonde, a waitress in a nearby café, who served Terry Thomas almost daily with his lunch. She knew him well. She said that she had seen him take a knife from his pocket and lunge it into the barman's back almost simultaneously with the undoubted assailant whom she also identified—and then she saw him run off. I froze as I listened to her evidence; it sounded so convincing. I decided that I needed more time before questioning her. I would leave her alone until trial.

Then another girl, a rather mousey creature, was called to give evidence to like effect. In cross-examination I determined that she was a close friend of the first girl, and I came to the conclusion that she was a 'camp follower' of hers who would do and say anything that the first girl, with whom she had discussed the case fully, wanted; a weak character, and a far less impressive witness. I was not afraid of her.

I gave endless thought as to how to tackle 'Blondie', and I still had no concerted plan when the case got to the Old Bailey. Her evidence, if true, was enough to convict Terry Thomas; and it had sounded so convincing in the Ipswich Magistrates' Court. But at least I had worried so much about her evidence that I knew every word of her deposition by heart. At the Old Bailey I felt that she was a little less confident, a bit nervous (perhaps on account of the rather formidable atmosphere of Court No 1 of the Central Criminal Court). And she said something slightly, but only slightly, different from what she had said in Ipswich. I pointed out the discrepancy. She got furious, 'Are you calling me a liar?' she shouted. The former cool, almost glacial, exterior had vanished.

'Why are you getting so angry?' I asked. 'This man is on his trial for murder.' And then I had a rare moment of inspiration, and asked a question that was in no way premeditated.

'The trouble with you is that you've got a colour prejudice, isn't it?'

'Well, I serve them, don't I?' answered the girl, curling her lip contemptuously. I looked at the jury, I saw most of them react with disgust to that disgusting reply, and I realised that Terry Thomas now had little to fear. I had asked a question to which I did not know the answer, but I believe that it won the case.

Later on I was to defend this self-same calm cool girl at Ipswich Quarter Sessions when she was accused of an assault occasioning actual bodily harm on a customer in her café—a West Indian . . .

Terry Thomas seemed to have been studying some law during his time on remand. Following his acquittal of murder, the taxi-driver returned to Ipswich, got very drunk that same night, and entered the police station shouting: 'I'm the Rainbow murderer. Arrest me!' When the station sergeant moved forward to do so, he exclaimed triumphantly: '*Autrefois acquit! Autrefois acquit!*' They decided to charge him with drunk and disorderly!

Even so, I do not believe that Terry Thomas was a Rainbow murderer. I think that it was just his natural arrogance and bravado asserting themselves after he had subdued them so successfully in the witness-box of the Old Bailey.

The other piece of advice that the 'old stagers' will give you, is: '*Never go on too long in cross-examination*'. In case my readers think that this chapter on cross-examination is going on too long I will reserve my comments and anecdotes on 'asking one question too many' until the next chapter.

9 When the questioning has to stop

'Don't ask too many questions.' This is the advice that every pupil master gives to his pupil, that everyone in articles who may venture into court will receive from his principal. It is emphasised so strongly by the 'old stagers' that there may even be a danger that the novice may not ask enough questions to ram home his point.

I was appearing in Croydon Magistrates' Court for a woman who was alleging desertion by her husband. The desertion was of the 'constructive' variety: he had made life unbearable for her because, she suspected, he wanted another woman to join him in the matrimonial home (although she was not in a position to prove this). The wife seemed a very pleasant sort of person; the husband something of a 'Smart Alec' (I hope that my liking for her and my dislike of him were not influenced by her having had the discernment to employ me as her counsel!) Under the old matrimonial law the court was always interested in the animus of the parties, particularly their willingness to resume cohabitation.

'Do you want your wife back?' I asked.

'The door is open', the husband replied.

'I do not think that the court is concerned with the state of the door', I insisted. 'Do you want her back?'

'There is nothing that I can see to prevent her coming back,' he answered.

Not only was his equivocation suspicious, but I wondered if he had really dressed so smartly that Friday afternoon merely to impress the Bench of Magistrates. So I chanced my arm.

'Good!' I said, 'then I shall advise your wife to return to the matrimonial home this evening—will you be there to welcome her?'

The terrible expression that came to his face made it clear that I was interfering with his immediate plans. 'If she comes back tonight', he said menacingly, 'I shall kill her.'

At rare moments like this during cross-examination one must sit down. One should not try to capitalise on the situation by further questioning. No other question and answer will be so effective. The better is the enemy of the good. But the point is that it was necessary to press on so far with the cross-examination to get that so revealing answer. If I had been content to leave it at 'the door is open' or his next answer, his real attitude would have been far less clear to the Bench.

Yet the 'old stagers' will tell you that far more cases have been lost by asking too many questions in cross-examination than in any other way (and they are right). I can think of many instances when I endangered a good case by asking too much, and I will recite the details of two cases that I clearly lost by this method.

One was another matrimonial, at North London, before the late Sir Frank Milton, before he became such a fine Chief Magistrate. The wife, asking for a separation order on the ground of her husband's persistent cruelty, complained: 'I've had bruises for years. Why, only last month I had a split lip.'

Her sister, who lived in the same house as the parties, was called to give corroborative evidence. 'I've seen bruises on my sister's legs for years', she said, but nothing about the split lip of a month earlier. I, acting for the husband, took a very stupid course. This was a witness who had done the respondent little harm. It would have been far better not to have cross-examined her at all, and in my closing address to have commented on how strange it was that the sister had said nothing of the split lip of the previous month. And the bruises on the wife's legs could perhaps be explained away in the case of a couple who, until a few weeks earlier, had been sharing the same bed. (Here the advice of the old stagers with which, as I said in my last chapter, I am not always in wholehearted agreement: 'Do not cross-examine a witness who has done you no harm', would have been good advice.) But I waded right in, only to drown. Under-estimating the tribunal—it was only the second or third time that I had appeared before Sir Frank—I wanted to emphasise already the point (which I am now quite sure that he would have noticed) that the sister had said nothing about the split lip. I proceeded to ask one of the most otiose (and dangerous) questions that can possibly be imagined.

'You say that your sister has been marked by her husband', I said, repeating the evidence (quite needlessly). 'I think you said that she'd had *bruises* for years.'

'Yes', she replied, 'and last month I remember she had a split lip.'

There was corroboration, and Sir Frank found persistent cruelty proved.

For years I had been thinking of writing a book on advocacy, on which topic I have been lecturing for nearly three and a half decades. In 1964, just when I had it all in my mind, Richard Du Cann produced his brilliant analysis *The Art of the Advocate* (published by Penguin)—and he was in my old Chambers, too! Indeed, he dedicates the book to 'QEB'. A decade or so later I had regirded my loins and got together all my material when, lo and behold! Sir David Napley, certainly the best known of solicitor advocates, came out with *The Technique of Persuasion* (Sweet & Maxwell), now in its third edition. Now I would not like you to think that I am complaining against either of these eminent advocates, each of whom had stolen my thunder: indeed I have so much for which to be grateful to each of them (in quite different ways) that for me to complain would be ungracious. But between them they delayed my getting into print for over twenty years! And then, just when I was gathering steam again in 1982 my friend and colleague Ronald Bartle wrote a single article entitled 'Sentencing and the Advocate' (1982) 146 JPN 246. It was an excellent article, very succinct, but not sufficient to deter me from producing my own material for yet another ten years! So I got started, and you are reading the results.

Both Richard Du Cann QC and Sir David Napley emphasise in their books the dangers of asking too many questions. Du Cann writes, in *The Art of the Advocate*: 'Prolonged cross-examination places unnecessary and often unfair strain on the witness and is a waste of public and private time and money'. (I appeared against him many times and he was never guilty of asking too many questions.) And I reproduce from memory two anecdotes recounted by Sir David of the disastrous results of asking too many questions.

An Army Officer was court-martialled for being drunk on duty on 30 April. The prosecution called his batman. He was a loyal servant and a reluctant witness who, if possible, wanted to say nothing against his officer, to whom he was devoted, and the prosecutor got nowhere in examination-in-chief. The defending officer would have been wise to leave well alone, but he thought it necessary to improve on this negative testimony—and he was dealing with a basically honest witness.

Q Is it right that when he came back from duty he seemed perfectly normal?
A Yes, sir.
Q He was walking quite normally?
A Yes, sir.
Q And he went to bed quite normally?
A Yes, sir.
Q And did he ask you to call him at the usual time?
A No, sir.
(At this point warning bells should have sounded in the cross-examiner's brain. If they did, he failed to hear them).
Q Oh, really. Didn't he?
A No, sir. He said I should call him early.
Q And did he say why you should call him early?
(This detail was quite unnecessary to the case).
A Yes, he said: 'Call me early, Mother dear, for I'm to be Queen of the May.'

The other case arose from an allegation of carnal

knowledge of a girl just under sixteen. Her evidence was corroborated by the testimony of a middle-aged farmer who had been watching the event some fifty yards or so away. The cross-examination went something like this (I don't know why, but I always imagine it to have happened in the West Country, with the farmer speaking with a rich Devonian accent):

Q Now, Mr Giles, I suppose when you were young, thirty years or so ago, you would sometimes be courting a young girl, eh?
A Aye, you be right.
Q And sometimes you would go with her hand-in-hand to a cornfield?
A Aye, you be right.
Q And then if it were a hot day, and you were tired, you would both lie down in the cornfield?
A Aye, you be right.
Q And, if the day were very hot, you might both remove some of your clothing?
A Aye, you be right.
Q And, if the girl were attractive, you would move closer to her?
A Aye, you be right.
Q And then when you were close together, a bit of kissing and cuddling might take place?
A Aye, you be right.
Q And someone watching what you were doing, from fifty yards or more away, might suspect that you were having carnal knowledge of that girl?
A Aye, and they'd be dead right!

Geoffrey Crispin QC was one of the best-known divorce practitioners of my days at the Bar. (He afterwards became Chairman of Hertford Quarter Sessions). He told the story of counsel who, carried away by his enthusiasm, went on too long with a cross-examination, with disastrous results. The allegation against a wife in divorce proceedings based on adultery was that she was promiscuous. In support of this suggestion a deaf, foreign lady who lived opposite the matrimonial home was called to give evidence of what she had seen. It soon became clear that she was malevolent towards the respondent and counsel sought to ridicule her evidence by hyperbole. He did this by raising the pitch of his voice with each question.

Q You say she had a lot of men coming to visit her. How many different men do you suggest visited her in the course of a week? Five?
A Yes, that's right.
Q Ten?
A Yes, that's right.
Q Fifteen?
A Yes, that's right.
Q Twenty?
A Yes, that's right.
Q Twenty-five?
A Yes, that's right.
Q Thirty?
A Yes, that's right.
Q (Very emphatic.) So she had *thirty different men* visiting her in a week?

The witness, obviously shocked and not having heard any of the previous questions, replied in astonishment: 'Did she?'

The next county to Hertford is Essex, where counsel prosecuting a burglar who had been on bail pending his trial made the triple error of employing heavy irony, being unduly pompous, and asking one question too many.

Q On the night in question when you were arrested you were wearing gloves?
A Yus.
Q The month was July?
A Yus.
Q They were woollen gloves?
A Yus.
Q Warm woollen gloves?
A Yus.
Q Would you care to tell the learned judge and the jury

just why you were wearing warm woollen gloves at night in the middle of July?

A Well, Mr Beeswax, I saw you coming into court this morning and you was carrying an umbrella, but it wasn't raining.

The jury liked him for it, and he was acquitted.

I have recited five cases where the cross-examination went wrong because it went on too long, as against just one where it was necessary to keep prodding to get the just and succcessful result, and I propose to give yet another instance of asking one question too many, because I think that the young barrister or solicitor is at least six times as likely to ask too many questions as he or she is to ask too few. In most of the other cases I have relied on my recollection, which may be fallible, but in this case I rely on a memory which is infallible, as the horror of this matter is deeply engraved in my soul. It was the case of *Allah Bux* v *Choudhury*, which was heard in the Shoreditch County Court (where I seem to have conducted a lot of my civil practice at the Bar) and I am so sure of my facts, because I was counsel for the plaintiff in that horrifying case.

By his particulars of claim Mr Allah Bux alleged that he had lent £400 to Mr Choudhury, who had never repaid it. By his defence Mr Choudhury admitted the loan, but averred that it had been repaid. I made a preliminary submission to Judge McMillan that on the face of the pleadings the burden of proof had passed to the defendant and therefore the defendant should open and give his evidence first—a useful tactic if a case may be borderline. The judge agreed and Mr Choudhury gave evidence-in-chief to this effect:

'I was driving along in my lorry and I saw Mr Allah Bux in the street and I thought "There is Mr Allah Bux to whom I owe £400". So I stopped my lorry and I got out and I gave £400 to Mr Allah Bux. Thank you.'

Crowther rose to cross-examine. I like to think that it

was a good cross-examination—up to a point. (All of this happened nearly forty years ago, so due allowance must be made for inflation in all the figures that are recited, perhaps by multiplying by ten to bring them up to today's values.)

Q I gather from what you just said that you are a lorry driver?
A Yes, please.
Q What do you earn as a lorry driver?
A £15 a week, please.
Q And what is your weekly rent or mortgage repayment?
A £3, please.
Q Are you married, Mr Choudhury?
A Yes, please.
Q And do you and your wife have any children?
A Yes, we have three lovely children.
Q How old is the oldest child?
A Seven, please.
Q Are your wife and children in this country, or in Pakistan?
A They are living here with me, please. We are a very happy family.
Q Does your wife work?
A No, the children are very young.
Q So, after your rent has been paid, you have only £12 a week for a family of five?
A Yes, it is a hard struggle, but somehow we manage.
Q Tell me, did you know that you were going to see Mr Allah Bux on the day about which you have told us?
A No, no. I told you, I was driving along in my lorry and I saw Mr Allah Bux . . .
Q Yes, we heard all that, but the point is that you did not expect to see him on that day?
A Not at all
Q And you just happened to have £400 on you at the time?
A Yes, please.

Q (uttered very solemnly). Tell me, Mr Choudhury, do you happen to have £400 on you now?

There was a pause, during which the witness drew a large wallet from his jacket pocket, and scattered £5 notes from it all over the witness-box in front of him, saying triumphantly: 'I have £700'.

That was another one that I lost.

When I was looking through *The Art of the Advocate* just before beginning to write this book, I noted that Richard Du Cann commented on the brevity of Sir Patrick Hastings' cross-examinations—with the notable exception of the *Laski* libel case—but he also complained of Sir Patrick's habit of including comment in questions which he said made Sir Patrick as a cross-examiner, on occasions, 'ruthless', 'unfair' and 'grossly discourteous'. Comment has no place in cross-examination. This question, which I once heard put during a criminal trial, was quite improper: 'Would not a well-dressed man like you be readily mistaken for a plain-clothes police officer?' It really contains two comments that may be based on false assumptions: (i) that the witness was well dressed, and (ii) that all plain clothes police officers are latter-day Beau Brummels. Both of these, if relevant, are matters that ought to be left to the opinion of the jury or the magistrates.

The worst sort of comment, as I have indicated in an earlier chapter, is the one in which the advocate expresses his personal opinion or feeling. To give an extreme example of how unfair and ill-advised this could be, let us assume that a young barrister of under a year's call finds himself defending a person on a serious charge at the Old Bailey (and, alas, it can happen). He concludes his closing address—which is the rightful place, and indeed the only place, for proper, pertinent comment, with these words:

'And finally, members of the jury, I ask you to acquit the defendant because I have spent a lot of time with him in conference and I am quite convinced that he is innocent.'

He could hardly complain if prosecuting counsel rose in his wrath and said: 'Members of the jury, I want to tell you that I have been prosecuting at this court for nearly a quarter of a century, and I have never come across anyone so obviously guilty as this defendant'.

No, neither of these grossly unfair expressions of personal opinion would be allowed by the judge. But likewise comment, whether personal or general, is quite inappropriate during cross-examination. I once saw a leading junior, who specialised in acting for insurance companies in accident cases, come completely unstuck through making a personal comment during his questioning of a plaintiff. He was a member of the Bar of great experience, who, as I afterwards discovered, was noted for his 'Barmanship'—the Bar's equivalent of Stephen Potter's 'Gamesmanship'.

The plaintiff, whom I was representing, had suffered grievous injuries at his place of work, but his cause of action against his employers was not strong. It looked very much as though he were the author of his own misfortune. I got to court early in the hope that the other side would offer to settle in a modest sum. I waited a long time and then my opponent's clerk appeared and introduced himself to me. 'I don't know if my governor will be coming on this case', he told me. 'He says it's such a winner from his point of view that he may not waste his time on it. He'll probably send along one of his pupils to cut his teeth on it.' Then—looking along the corridor, where he was anticipating the well-timed appearance: 'No, sir, you're unlucky today, here he comes. The Great Man has obviously decided to do it himself. Bad luck, sir.'

And the 'Great Man' appeared and offered me a sum so derisory (to use the term of which trade union officials are so fond) that, despite my misgivings about the case, I rejected it out of hand.

The case was heard by Nield J who had only just been appointed as a High Court judge, although he had been sitting as a judge for many years in Manchester Crown Court. The plaintiff did not shine in examination-in-chief. The Great Man rose to cross-examine. With almost his first question he got an answer which pleased him. 'Huh!

That's just what I thought you'd say', he remarked contemptuously.

Mr Justice Nield, normally the most courteous of judges, descended on him furiously.

'How dare you make such a comment in my court!' he exclaimed. 'I do not care in the slightest what you may think. Your opinion is of no interest to me. I do not expect counsel of your experience to resort to such tactics. Kindly do not behave in such a way again.'

The Great Man crumpled, and crumbled, and murmured and mumbled. I do not think that any judge had rebuked him like that for years. None of the rest of his cross-examination was in the least effective—nor indeed was any of the remainder of his conduct of the case—and, to my considerable surprise (and the delight of my crippled client) we won the case, with full damages. I do not think that we would have done so if my opponent had not uttered those unwise words: 'That's just what I thought you'd say'. Yet how much gratuitous comment in the guise of questions does one hear in court, especially in the magistrates' court? I cannot stress too much that in every court the only place for comment—strong but impersonal (never personal)—is in the advocate's closing address.

Cross-examination is generally regarded as the most important aspect of the advocate's art—but never underestimate the importance of examination-in-chief and of a good plea in mitigation—so, having devoted two chapters to the subject, may I summarise them with some DOs and DON'Ts for cross-examination? In some cases they will overlap (with a DO being almost the direct opposite of a DON'T).

The DOs:

(1) DO put your case in cross-examination.
(2) DO put it early.
(3) DO have a plan, a pattern and a purpose. Every question must have an aim in view.
(4) DO think carefully about what your first and your last question will be.
(5) DO be fair in all your questioning.

(6) DO be courteous.
(7) DO ask brief, crisp, meaningful questions designed to keep up the pressure.
(8) DO put in character, when you safely can, in criminal cases in cross-examination (as well as, later on, in chief).
(9) DO appear earnest and sincere as you cross-examine.
(10) DO be prepared to be flexible, if an unexpected witness is called, or if matters take an unexpected turn.

The DON'Ts

(1) DON'T aim too high when you cross-examine.
(2) DON'T generally cross-examine a witness who has done you no harm.*
(3) DON'T generally ask a question to which you yourself do not know the answer.*
(4) DON'T put previous convictions to a witness unless you hold the memorandum of convictions, or the witness's Criminal Record Office form, in your hand.
(5) DON'T forget that if you cross-examine as to credit, you are bound by the answers.
(6) DON'T be a bully or pompous.
(7) DON'T ask double or treble questions, or long rambling questions which include subordinate clauses.
(8) DON'T include comment in questions or express your own opinions.
(9) DON'T ask more than about three questions when prosecuting in a driving case.
(10) DON'T ask too many questions.

**Note*:
But remember, there may be exceptions to these two rules where you ask the unexpected witness the unexpected question, or where you feel that it is essential at all costs to get at the truth of a matter (especially in respect of a witness's motives).

10 To bail—or not to bail?

When I went into court as a magistrate I never knew what to expect. This was one of the joys of my job. It could also be one of its horrors. Certainly when I went into court on 17 May 1978 I had no idea what was awaiting me. A glance down the register showed that one of about fifty cases that morning concerned a nineteen year old youth who had been charged with two offences of sending a 'noxious substance through the post contrary to the Post Office Act 1953'. They were slightly unusual charges and I wondered what they involved. About an hour later, I was to find out.

The defendant worked in a factory. He had become enamoured of a young girl who also worked there. His love was unrequited—indeed the girl was quite unaware of it, for, being shy, he had never directly expressed his feelings to her. However, he had sent her a present of a bottle of perfume, together with an anonymous letter in which he had declared his love. Unfortunately she had shown this present to colleagues in the works canteen, and read the letter out, and there had been a lot of ribald laughter. He had been present when this happened, but he did not join in the merriment. He decided to take a terrible revenge.

That night he enticed the cat of an elderly woman neighbour into his bathroom by offering it food. Then he drowned the cat in the bath and cut off its tail, which he sent to the girl through the post. The tail was accompanied by an unsavoury note, signed 'Psycho'. A day or two later he found a live frog in his garden. He put it in a registered envelope and sent it to the girl with another anonymous note saying: 'I killed my mummy and daddy. Heh, heh, heh!' The Post Office was really in form that week, because when the registered letter was opened the frog jumped out, alive and well. The girl was terrified.

Nearly a hundred people worked in that factory and they all had to be interviewed before the enquiries centred on the defendant. Eventually he admitted the offences and made a long written statement in which he expressed his intention to kill the girl with an axe, and boasted that he had killed two sheep and hung their entrails on trees in Richmond Park. He said that it had taken him two hours to kill one sheep, which he had finally finished off by ripping out its heart. The police found the axe at his home and had no doubt of the truth of his claim relating to the sheep. The press were right when they reported that women in the public gallery gasped when they heard the details recited. They were not alone in gasping. The officer in charge of the case opposed bail on the ground that he had no doubt at all that if granted bail the defendant would try to kill the girl. He had told the officer that he wanted bail for this very reason. On the face of it, it did not seem a very suitable case for bail. But there were difficulties.

The Bail Act 1976 had come into operation just a month earlier. It provided a statutory presumption in favour of bail. Then it divided offences into two categories, imprisonable and non-imprisonable. In so far as imprisonable offences are concerned the defendant need not be granted bail if he falls within one of the exceptions to the right to bail contained in Pt I to the First Schedule of the Bail Act, of which the most usual are contained in Para 2, viz that there are substantial grounds for believing that the defendant would:

(a) fail to surrender to custody, or
(b) commit an offence while on bail, or
(c) interfere with witnesses or otherwise obstruct the course of justice.

As to non-imprisonable offences the position is governed by Pt II of the First Schedule and the limitations on the right to bail are much more severe. Basically the defendant can be refused bail for a non-imprisonable offence only if he has previously failed to surrender to custody when granted bail and the court is prepared to certify that in view of that failure the defendant would fail to turn up in this new matter.

That did not apply in my case, as the defendant had no previous convictions. (I hesitate to use the phrase 'was of previous good character'.)

In its unavailing efforts to reduce the prison population the Home Office had inserted into the Criminal Law Act 1977 provisions rendering a number of offences formerly punishable by imprisonment non-imprisonable and sending noxious matter through the post was one of them. Formerly it had carried three months' imprisonment and/or a small fine. Now imprisonment for this offence when tried summarily had been abolished and the maximum fine increased to £1,000. The effect of these two recent changes in the law appeared to be that this defendant was entitled to be released on bail. Counsel, doing his duty to his client, argued this with tact, skill and force.

I did not see it that way. I was never a magistrate who made a habit of lying awake at night worrying about my cases, but I would have been unable to sleep if I had set that young man free to kill that innocent, frightened girl. There was a possible way out of the dilemma which I rejected. Paragraph 3 to Pt II of the Second Schedule says: 'The defendant need not be granted bail if the court is satisfied that the defendant should be kept in custody for his own protection.' It was not for *his* protection that I wanted him kept in custody, but for the girl's protection. I do not think that courts should have to resort to hypocrisy to do what is obviously right. It is bad enough that we have to certify that we are considering disqualification in order to issue a warrant to force a recalcitrant driver to produce his licence at court. The offence is a minor one: travelling at 41 mph in a built-up area, or parking within the limits of a pedestrian crossing. No magistrates' court considers disqualification for such trivial motoring offences. But when, three or more four-weekly adjournments have failed to produce the defendant's licence, we have either to let the offence go without endorsing the licence (which is unfair to those who do produce their licences at the right time), or to go through the mental gymnastics of imagining that the defendant has nine penalty points on his licence and therefore now qualifies to be considered for disqualification, and that this is why he is shy about producing it. Then when eventually the defendant does appear on warrant (many months after the case was proved against him) it turns out that his licence is in the Swansea washing-machine! I hate these ruses to which we must subject ourselves to try to do justice. Now even more restrictions have been imposed on the exercise of the court's discretion by ss 153–155 of the Criminal Justice Act 1988. Section 153 actually inserts a new para (9A) into Pt I of the First Schedule to the Bail Act 1976 requiring courts to give their reasons for *granting* bail in certain serious cases. If at first sight that looks like a reversal of the statutory presumption in favour of bail we have the assurance of a Home Office official Mr N S Benger, that this is not the case (*Justice of the Peace*, 24 February 1990).

But I do not really blame the Home Office officials who dreamed up the First Schedule to the Bail Act. They could hardly have foreseen a situation so gruesome and so bizarre as that which was to confront me a month after the Act came into operation. But things so often seem to go wrong when Parliament attempts needlessly to fetter the discretion of the courts. Surely the better course is to appoint judges and magistrates who can be trusted to exercise their discretion judicially and fairly and leave them to get on with the job. I venture to think that no statutory provisions could ever cater for my 'cat's tail' case. Eventually the difficulty was overcome by the defendant's being further charged with causing criminal damage to the cat! This, too, was highly artificial, almost laughable if the case had not been so horrific—but criminal damage to the property of another does still carry three months' imprisonment in a magistrates' court, so once the defendant was charged with that there was no doubt that he could be kept in custody under the provisions of Para 2(b) of Pt I of the

First Schedule of the Bail Act 1976; viz that there were substantial grounds for believing that the defendant, if released on bail, would commit an offence—murder (or manslaughter)— because he said he would. The cat, as I have said, had belonged to the old lady next door. What could have been done if it had been a stray?

In the controversy that followed my decision not to follow the strict letter of the Bail Act, help was forthcoming from an unexpected quarter. The Editor of the *Justice of the Peace* wrote that one could not fail to have sympathy with me in my dilemma—a dilemma which the draftsmen of the Bail Act had not foreseen. I wrote to thank him for his unsolicited support—and from that correspondence the idea of the first edition of this book grew. So from my point of view at least it was 'an ill-wind . . .'.

The young man remained in custody until the Crown Court judge sent him to Broadmoor. For the surprisingly happy ending of this story see my most recent book *Look What's on the Bench!*

Was it really necessary for Parliament to provide in terms by s 4 of the Act that 'A person to whom this section applies shall be granted bail, except as provided in Schedule 1 to this Act'? Was it really necessary to lay down a statutory presumption of bail? Although I do remember one court in the 1960s where the chairman always used to say. 'If the police say there will be no bail, there will be no bail' (that court at least had the virtue of consistency), I would have thought that such an attitude had disappeared by the mid-1970s after a decade of compulsory training for justices. Certainly all the justices in the courts with which I have been associated since I became a magistrate have seemed to try to be fair and reasonable over bail, and were applying the presumption in favour of it long before it was expressed in any Act of Parliament. My own approach before the Bail Act was to ask the officer in charge of the case: 'Tell me, is this defendant at the moment in any of the following positions: on probation, subject to a conditional discharge, subject to a suspended sentence or already on bail in respect of any other matter?' If the answer to that question was 'yes', then my own mental presumption in favour of bail would swing the other way. (Admittedly the defendant in my 'cat's tail' case would not have fallen into any of those categories, but I think there is a residue of cases in which one should be prepared to leave it to the good sense of the Bench to see that right and justice are done.) Whilst, of course, as is so often urged, the defendant has not yet been convicted of the new offence and so is innocent of it, I cannot but in this instance by analogy go along with Lady Bracknell's rather cynical observation: 'To lose one parent, Mr Worthing, may be a misfortune. To lose both savours of carelessness.'

Since the Bail Act, contested applications for bail have been much more numerous and have taken much longer. They are one of the reasons for greater delays in getting cases heard in magistrates' courts. I do not complain of this. The question of bail for the unconvicted defendant—especially if he may in reality be innocent of the offence—is obviously of great importance in any society that cherishes the liberty of the subject. But I do beg advocates to keep a sense of proportion in making these applications.

I think it is fair to assume that now, several years after the Bail Act came into operation, most courts have a working knowledge of its philosophy. It is true that in the early days there were some difficulties over comprehending the Act. I remember that when it was still in the form of a Bill I was asked to lecture on its implications to the Surrey Justices. I found that I could not understand it. I pondered over it for hours. Then I consulted my colleague at West London (now Her Honour Judge Nina Lowry). Her keen mind quickly saw through the difficulty. She told me: 'If you will read Clause 6 before Clause 5 it will begin to make sense', and I found that this simple technique did work, enabling me to give the lecture. (I cannot now be sure of the number of the two clauses, but there were two that had to be transposed. That ambiguity, at least, which had cost me hours of anxiety over interpretation, was ironed out when the Bill became an Act!)

So do make your application briefly. Surely a strong bail application should not normally last longer than a good plea in mitigation, which can usually be achieved in five minutes in a magistrates' court. I have on occasions, when advocates have gone on too long, said that I would put their applications for bail over to 4 pm. (This does seem to have the effect of enabling them to condense the rest of their argument into one sentence.) On one such occasion, when a solicitor had been arguing that his client, allegedly involved in a conspiracy to sell heroin worth millions of pounds on the streets of London, should have bail—a proposition to which, admittedly, few courts would readily agree—and had been addressing me for nearly half an hour, I noted, when I put the remainder of his application over to 4 pm, the other solicitors and barristers who were waiting to come on nodding and smiling with relief. Be realistic about bail! You must do your duty to your present client, but your future clients (if any) will not be helped by the Bench's recollection of your previous futile and seemingly interminable application.

Most advocates in my view concentrate too much on Para 2(a) to Pt I of the First Schedule of the Bail Act and not enough on 2(b). The objection to bail brought under Para 2(c), namely that the defendant if granted bail would interfere with witnesses or with the course of justice is difficult to counter, because it is so nebulous in its nature. Sometimes it is true, and then cross-examination of the police officer tends to make the defendant's involvement in the offence charged seem much worse. At other times it may be used by a wily officer to keep someone whom he does not like in custody when there are not really solid grounds for doing so. This objection to bail has to be handled with great care by the defending advocate, but it is worth emphasising that this vague allegation must always be speculative, and courts should be governed by firm evidence in important matters and not by speculation—even though the police are sometimes proved right in their surmises.

Paragraph 2(a), of course, relates to the Court having substantial grounds for believing that the defendant will not attend his trial. Contrary to popular belief some defendants who are granted bail do not appear to stand their trials. During a four-week stint at the Crown Court a few years ago, I found that there were very few days on which I was able to start on time because very few defendants turned up to face their trials, although the gap in the list was sometimes filled after half an hour or so by one of the 'floaters'. The only survey that I have ever carried out at West London of non-appearances in answer to bail covered a period of three months during which 34 per cent of those granted bail did not appear. (I think it is only fair to add that these included some 'drunks' pleading Not Guilty when they were subject to conditional discharges for being drunk, and also that West London is certainly not typical of the country as a whole, being the apotheosis of 'bed-sitter land'. Those fine old Victorian houses in Earls Court are now, in the main, cheap hotels into which local authorities—often from far outside the Royal Borough of Kensington—put people from all over Britain, four to a room for bed and breakfast, when they can think of no other way to satisfy their statutory obligation to house them.) A passionate plea for bail was made to me some years ago by one of Sir David Napley's partners on behalf of a young client of that firm facing a serious drugs charge. The basis of the application was that this young man was a champion cyclist, about to set off on an international cycling competition around the world, and that I should let him do this for the honour of Britain. This plea stirred my patriotic fervour, and I allowed him bail, and directed that he should keep his passport so as to cycle through many frontiers waving the British flag, but, alas, I fear that he must have had a puncture somewhere near the Golden Triangle, for he has not been seen in this country since.

One of the less attractive arguments frequently advanced for bail goes somewhat as follows: 'He has a good bail record. You will see that he has seventeen previous convictions, all for serious offences, and there is no record of his ever having failed to appear to answer to his bail in the past.' I must confess that I would like the defendant much more if he had not committed any of those offences. A closer scrutiny of the record often reveals that some convictions were so close together that it is most unlikely that the defendant was remanded on bail at all. The defendant who does not turn up fails to do so for a number of reasons: (a) he is ill, or genuinely has some other good excuse; (b) he is casual and has forgotten all about it; (c) he is diligent, and has studied the list and does not like the particular judge or magistrate assigned to try his case; or (d) he is frightened. His failure to turn up is a confounded nuisance. If he is on legal aid, and the case is at the Crown Court, and there is no 'floater' available to take his place (perhaps because all the 'floaters' have also failed to appear), the fact of his non-appearance may cost the tax-payer hundreds of pounds (but less in the magistrates' courts). Worse still, the prosecution witnesses may get fed up and fail to turn up on the next occasion, when the defendant has been arrested on a warrant and so that trial may also be abortive; or indeed he may be acquitted for lack of evidence. So the objection under Para 2(a) does deserve serious consideration.

But far more important, surely, is the objection under Para 2(b). Every magistrate, lay or stipendiary, is a justice of the peace. King Edward III created this office in 1361 in order to make leading citizens responsible for the preservation of the peace. Are they fulfilling that function if they allow professional criminals to go free for long periods to commit further crimes before they are finally brought to justice?

Lord Hailsham once criticised the 'grave error' of justices in Hull who granted bail to a man awaiting trial for two rapes and one attempted rape and who, whilst on bail, murdered another woman. He said that he 'would be slow to grant bail when the charge was murder, attempted murder, rape or attempted rape, or wounding.' No doubt his views are reflected in the new provisions of s 153 of the Criminal Justice Act 1988. He went on: 'Magistrates should look at the strength of the prosecution case. The stronger it was, the more they should hesitate. They should also think twice if there were previous convictions.' Yet in *R* v *Vernege* [1982] 1 All ER 403, Dunn LJ commented that nowadays it was not uncommon for people even on charges of murder to be granted bail on their committal. But, he pointed out, in such cases, it was often in the defendant's own interests that he be remanded in custody for examination by the prison doctor for the doctor to consider whether the defendant's state of mind might lead to a defence of diminished responsibility.

A Court of Criminal Appeal presided over long ago by Lord Goddard roundly condemned justices who had granted bail to a professional burglar pending his appearance at a higher court, thereby enabling him to commit many more burglaries so as to 'set his family up' during the period that he anticipated being away. These sentiments have been echoed many times recently by leading judges in the Court of Appeal (Criminal Division), who have felt that the justices' duty to preserve the peace (the peace of mind, the peace in homes of their fellow citizens) over-rode the interests of the professional criminal. But who is to be regarded as a professional burglar? And how much regard should we have to the statistics that suggest that there is now a burglary in Britain every six seconds and that only about one in eleven is cleared up? My own attitude is to look at the previous record of the defendant who is accused of burglary and if he has two or more previous convictions for that offence in the last five years I regard him, *prima facie*, as a professional, and therefore to be refused bail unless there are very special extenuating circumstances. But one factor that must be taken into account is the strength of the case against him. This is something that Lord Hailsham said ought to be investigated by the court on every application for bail. I find that sometimes advocates get very upset when, following a s 6(2) committal, I say 'Well, I see that your client left his finger prints all over the house that was ransacked and that he had made a complete written confession to the police and in addition has initialled every question and answer of a prolonged interview'. Some advocates will suggest that I am not playing the game, as this is a committal 'without consideration of the evidence'. This does not apply to the question of bail. On the other hand if the case against the defendant is weak, depending on the fleeting identification of one observer who did not know the defendant before, or on the testimony of a witness who might be inspired by malice, of course, the defending advocate is right to emphasise such matters, whatever the record of the defendant, because he is likely to get off at his trial, and it is not desirable that people who are likely to be acquitted on the merits of the case should be kept in custody, whatever they may have done in the past. (I am not impressed, by the way, with figures of people who have been kept in custody but then not given a custodial sentence, because so often when there is a remand for reports with a view to, say, a sentence in a Young Offender Institute, favourable accounts will come back from both the Probation Officer and the Prisoner Governor and then it would be cruel as well as otiose to impose any custodial measure when a probation order or community service would now suffice.)

The court's duty to keep the peace can sometimes be satisfied, in the case of a young defendant, by his parent or guardian agreeing to enter into a surety for the defendant's good behaviour for a fixed period (usually a year, because the High Court has said that this is the maximum desirable period, and it will cover the period of most committals on bail—even in London). I used this method very often with youngsters who have been in a lot of trouble, but it is right to say that some of my stipendiary colleagues do not approve of it. I think it is particularly effective when the young defendant may feel a sense of gratitude and loyalty to his surety, or where the father, perhaps, is a criminal who has been employing his son to commit crimes, and then realises that the end of the road has been reached in respect of this particular offspring. It does not always work, however. In one case where I was considering a surety for good behaviour as a condition of bail (which I believe is legal under the Bail Act, though others doubt it) I asked a father if he would risk £100 on his son being of good behaviour for the next year. He looked at me contemptuously and asked: 'What do you think I am? Stupid?' It's a wise father who knows his own child.

If the magistrates decide to commit for sentence under s 38 of the Magistrates' Courts Act 1980, do not waste time applying for bail, because the High Court has said that the magistrates should not grant it. By committing for sentence the magistrates are saying that their own powers of sentence, normally six months' imprisonment, are insufficient. To grant bail in such circumstances, when threatening a defendant with a sentence almost inevitably in excess of six months would be an open invitation to the defendant to abscond. I have only once granted a defendant bail when committing for sentence under s 38 (or its predecessor—s 29) and the circumstances there were most unusual. So avoid bail applications on committals for sentence, please!

Whilst the advocate should always discover beforehand from the prosecution what is their attitude to bail, this is by no means conclusive. If it were, there would be no point in the magistrates adjudicating on bail applications, and the way would be open to bribery on this all-important question of bail. The police, in my view, are fairly shrewd about bail, but it is possible for a police officer vindictively to resist bail because a defendant has not been 'co-operative', or not to oppose bail because he does not want to be thought harsh or oppressive, or just because he is lazy. Nothing annoys me more in court than for a police officer, who is often called to express his opinions in serious cases, to say: 'There's no objection to bail, Your Worship' (or even worse, 'The defendant can have bail, Your Worship') 'if he provides two sureties each in the sum of £250 and reports nightly at his local police station'. I regard that as a gross usurpation of the magistrates' function, and I have been known to invite the officer concerned to take my place on the Bench, since he appears already to have made the decision. The worst case of this kind that I can remember occurred many years ago when three villains made their first appearance before me charged with armed robbery. The Detective-Sergeant in the case said, 'There's no objection to bail, Your Worship, with two sureties each in the sum of £500'. Then he added, enthusiastically, 'I've got the sureties here, and I'll call them if I may'. None of those defendants got bail. The attitude of the prosecution is one factor, but not the deciding factor, on the question of whether the defendant should be granted bail. The ultimate responsibility must lie with the Bench, and magistrates and advocates should never forget this.

One of the arguments most frequently advanced against the granting of bail is that the defendant is likely to abscond because he is 'NFA' (of 'no fixed abode'). Whilst I appreciate that this does make it difficult for the police to discover his whereabouts if he fails to attend, I do not think that this should be a conclusive argument against his having bail. The fact that a person has no home does not mean that he or she has no honour. One of my favourite 'regulars' at West London, some years ago, was the late, much-lamented Paddy Nolan, NFA. One day he surprised us all by pleading Not Guilty to some trivial charge. The policeman opposed bail on the ground that Mr Nolan might not turn up as he was of no fixed abode. Mr Nolan was most indignant: 'Of course I'll turn up, Mr Crowther', he asserted. 'You know me. I'm a man of my convictions!' He got bail!

Just as the question of who should be granted bail is a matter for the magistrates and not for the police, so is the question of who is suitable to stand as surety, both for the defendant's reappearance and for his good behaviour, and any conflict on this point must be settled by the court. I do not subscribe to the view that a person is unsuitable as a surety merely because he has a criminal conviction some ten or twenty years ago. On the other hand I would not usually accept wives (either of the conventional or the common law variety) as sureties—either for attendance or good behaviour—because I think that the emotional pressure on the lady concerned must be too great for her to refuse, and if the man did abscond, or commit another offence, what court would have the heart to estreat the money from the deserted or deceived wife?

Not so long ago a person seeking the writ of habeas corpus could apply for it to every judge of the Queen's Bench Division, until he found one prepared to grant it, or exhausted the list. In those days there were about a dozen

Queen's Bench judges. This is no longer possible, which is just as well, there now being more judges of the Queen's Bench Division than Metropolitan Stipendiary Magistrates. However, until recently the same principle seemed to apply to bail applications. The fact that a Bench a week later was differently constituted was deemed by many advocates to justify a full fresh application for bail. The former clerk to the Nottingham Justices, who has himself sat as a Deputy Metropolitan Stipendiary Magistrate, took a robust view of these repeated applications and strongly advised his justices not to entertain renewed applications unless there were a substantial change of circumstances. The *Nottingham Justices* case (*R* v *Nottingham JJ, ex parte Davies* (1980) 144 JP 233) was taken by local solicitors to the Divisional Court, and the clerk's view prevailed, so that now there could be no second application for bail unless a real change of circumstances can be shown. The effect of this decision—and its beneficial effect in shortening lists in magistrates' courts—has since been watered down by a more recent judgment that once it is established that there is a change of circumstances the Bench must hear the whole application *de novo* and this has been further blurred by s 154 of the Criminal Justice Act 1988. I have always taken the view (even after *Nottingham Justices*) that when a defendant is committed for trial, the committal itself justifies a fresh bail application, because there is a change of circumstances in that the defendant in custody is now unlikely to appear before a court again for far longer than eight days.

Do not forget in appropriate cases to ask for sureties to be made continuous, as this may save them from the inconvenience of attending court or a police station again, and the defendant from the hardship of spending a few hours, or even a night, in a prison cell. It is now possible for magistrates, even on a first hearing in their court, where a defendant elects trial by jury, to say that sureties shall be continuous until the trial of the matter at the Crown Court.

In 1972 the Chief Magistrate of Trinidad and Tobago invited me to sit with him in this court when the notorious murderer 'Michael X' appeared before him. He remanded the defendant in custody for four weeks. I was surprised at this. He told me that it was possible if the defendant was represented and both he and his advocate agreed. I thought this was a good idea. London's traffic had been disrupted too often by the posses of police who for security reasons accompanied the Krays and the Richardson gang to Bow Street week after week. I suggested it to the Chief Metropolitan Magistrates (Sir Frank Milton). He agreed that it was a good idea. It was proposed to introduce it into the Criminal Law Act 1977. But the House of Lords threw it out. They thought it an infringement of the liberty of the subject. But now something very similar has appeared in the Criminal Justice Act 1982, where it is provided that a person aged over seventeen who has been remanded in custody before conviction may be further remanded without being brought before the court if he has consented to this course and not withdrawn his consent, if he is legally represented, and there have been not more than two remand hearings in his absence. Further provisions of a similar nature are to be found in s 155 of the Criminal Justice Act 1988. Trinidad seems to be replacing Manchester (but not, I hope, weatherwise). In suitable cases do assist the court by agreeing to this course and not insisting on otiose appearances.

So some would say that there is nothing new under the sun. Long before the *Nottingham Justices* case—indeed long before the Bail Act 1976—stipendiary magistrates were insisting on a change of circumstances being shown before they were prepared to hear a further application for bail. There were many defendants in the Richardson gang case. All had their separate legal representatives. I was one of them, until Charlie Richardson sacked me because our views on how the case should be conducted seemed to differ substantially. (A book by him on the duty of the advocate would make interesting reading.) But until that happened I was one of those who went along to Bow Street week after week to try to get bail. It was not an enjoyable experience. The magistrate who was assigned to the matter got visibly weary of these repeated applications. So one day he asked each of us in turn, very abruptly: 'Any change in circumstances since last week?' When each of us in turn replied 'No', he said curtly: 'Then bail is refused'. This went on until he came to the last defendant, who on this occasion was represented by a pupil, his master being engaged elsewhere on even more important business. 'Any change in circumstances?' enquired the magistrate. 'Yes, sir', replied the pupil 'there are seven matters that I wish to call to your attention.' 'Seven!' exclaimed the magistrate, visibly changing colour. 'Then get on with your seven points.' Facing the magistrate, and counting them out on his fingers, the young advocate said slowly: 'Tuesday, Wednesday, Thursday, Friday, Saturday, Sunday, Monday . . .'

The rest of us, while admiring his courage, put our hands over our ears to protect the drums from the anticipated explosion.

11 The use of law books and law reports

The present Chief Magistrate said at a meeting of lay justices that I once attended that the stipendiary always approaches everything from behind, so I will deal first with Law Reports. They can be divided into three categories, according to the period they cover.

(1) *The Year Books* These are so old that they really belong to legal history, a subject concerning which I have always been profoundly ignorant. Only once in nearly forty years in the profession have I needed to refer to a Year Book. On that occasion I borrowed it, after obtaining the authority of a Bencher, from the library of an Inn of Court and took it with me to Suffolk to argue an archaic point of law before an elderly county court judge. On its way up to the Bench the usher dropped the volume, and some of the parchment pages dissolved in dust, which is why you will not often see me in the library of my Inn. You will have gathered that the Year Books are not often referred to nowadays, so I propose to say no more about them.

(2) *The Old Reports* Covering the period from 1440–1865. These were the results of private enterprise in the days when nationalisation (and rationalisation) were unknown. These reports appear under the initials of the reporters, for example:

B & Ad = Barnewall and Adolphus
C & P = Carrington and Payne
Esp = Espinasse

This casual method of reporting did not meet with the unqualified approval of the judges. In 1704 Chief Justice Holt fumed: 'See the inconvenience of these scrambling reports. They will make us appear to posterity for a parcel of blockheads'. While Lord Lyndhurst was to complain of one such reporter: 'I hear that he was accustomed to slumber over his notebook'.

Of all these private reporters Espinasse, who reported from 1793 to 1807, seems to have been the least popular with the judges, for Chief Baron Pollock declared: 'He heard only half of what went on in court, and he reported the other half', while Maule J expressed himself much more bluntly: 'I do not care for Espinasse, or any other ass'.

It is always dangerous, even nowadays, to rely on headnotes as authority without reading the whole of the judgments, for the headnote is only the reporter's summary of the judgment and is not always accurate. What, for example, would a kilt-swirling, sporran-bearing Scottish Nationalist make of this headnote to a case by a reporter called Lowndes? 'Possession of trousers in Scotland evidence of larceny in England'.

The fact is that law reporting up to nearly the middle of the last century was for the most part unreliable and it will be rare for the young solicitor or barrister to appear in a magistrates' or county court armed with an authority before 1837.

(3) *The New Reports* These began officially in 1865 when the Incorporated Council of Law Reporting came into being and undertook responsibility for '*THE LAW REPORTS*'. These have official sanction because they are submitted to the judges for revision (revision of the wording, of course—not of the substance of the judgments) by the judges themselves. The judges pass the transcripts before they are released. For this reason they are preferred to all other reports and, if a case is reported in several places, it is the 'Law Report' that should be produced in court (unless the head of Chambers or the senior partner has taken it elsewhere). But the way had been prepared for these new reports by the *Justice of the Peace Reports*, the

first of the really reliable reports, which had begun in 1837. These excellent reports still appear monthly or fortnightly specialising now in criminal law and local government reports. They too derive from the judges' checked transcripts.

The Law Reports began with eleven different series of reports, which have been gradually whittled down to four.

The all-important Judicature Act 1873-75, which fused the old rivals of the Common Law Courts and the Courts of Equity into the Supreme Court of Judicature, reduced the number of courts, with the result that the eleven different series of reports were reduced to six.

In 1881 the Court of Exchequer and the Court of Common Pleas were assimilated into the Queen's Bench Division, and so the series was reduced to four. So, bearing in mind that the New Reports came into existence in 1865, we have eleven series of reports for eleven years (the Judicature Act 1873-75 came into operation on 1 January 1876); six series of reports for six years; and four thereafter, since 1881. In 1891 the simplified practice began of referring to the cases by the year in which they were reported rather than by the year in which judgment was given (often the previous year). Prior to that if a date appeared in square brackets, eg [1890], this indicated the year of the report, whereas if it appeared in rounded brackets, eg (1889) that indicated the year of the decision, but fortunately this has not been a problem since 1891. Up to 1890 reports from the Queen's Bench Division are correctly abbreviated as 'QBD' Reports: thereafter as 'QB' (or 'KB') Reports. From 1881 to 1970 the four series of Law Reports were:

(1) *Appeal Cases (AC)* in which are reported only the speeches of the Law Lords and the judges who are members of the Privy Council.

(2) *Queen's Bench Division (QB—sometimes KB)* of which there are often two or three or four volumes for a year. So, if you wanted to refer the court to a judgment of a member of the Court of Appeal in *Leaf* v *The International Galleries* (which is unlikely, since the

question of innocent representation is now covered by statute law) you would say: 'May I refer your Lordship to the judgment of Lord Justice Denning in *Leaf and the International Galleries 1950 King's Bench Division Volume 2 page 86 at page 90?*' You would *not* refer his Lordship to 'the judgment of Denning, LJ in *Leaf* v *International Galleries* 1950 KB Vol 2 p 86 at p 90'. NEVER use initials or abbreviations in court. (Don't ever talk to magistrates about 'tics', although the police will always do so. I once sat in a traffic court in which an officer started to give the registration number of a vehicle as 'Hotel, Yankee, Romeo'—a horrifying if romantic antithesis to initials.)

(3) *Chancery Division (Ch)* These Reports usually run to only one volume per year. Could this be because Chancery litigation is so expensive?

(4) *Probate (P)* for Probate, Divorce and Admiralty matters. The connection between Divorce and Admiralty jurisdiction was never particularly clear. The view that it derived from a sailor having a girl in every port is not generally accepted. At all events one disgruntled judge who was assigned to the 'PDA' complained that he felt that he had 'one foot in the sea and another in a sewer'. Some attempt to produce a little more logic in the distribution of labour arose from the Administration of Justice Act 1970, which established the Family Division and sent all *contentious* Probate matters to the Chancery Division and all Admiralty matters to the Queen's Bench Division. The result of this is that since 1972 there have been no Probate (P) Reports as such, but there has been instead a series of Reports for the Family Division.

(5) *Family Division (Fam)* The law in relation to divorce and family matters having changed drastically in 1969.

So now the four series are AC, QB, Ch and Fam (if you will forgive the initials).

Appeal Cases do not report, as one might suppose they would, cases heard in the Court of Appeal. These are printed in the series of the Division of the Court from which they emanated. A Court of Appeal decision from a Queen's Bench judge is therefore to be found in the *Queen's Bench Reports*. A distinctive feature of the Law Reports is that counsels' arguments are summarised at the beginning of the Reports.

This same Incorporated Society of Law Reporting used to publish *Weekly Notes (WN)* but ceased doing so in 1953 when these were superseded by *Weekly Law Reports* (WLR). These are bound annually in three volumes, of which Volumes 2 and 3 finish up in the Law Reports but Volume 1 does not. So, in Volume 1 of the *Weekly Law Reports* you will find some of the reported decisions which are regarded as less important than the others. The *Weekly Law Reports* contain virtually all of the important reportable cases. The aspiring advocate who wishes always to be abreast of the law (and who can afford to be!) should consider taking out a subscription to *Weekly Law Reports* (and reading them) or, alternatively, to the *All England Reports*, of which more later. But even with the Law Reports, the provision of adequate reports below the Court of Appeal can be a hit and miss affair. Several times I was in the High Court conducting cases of momentous significance (or so they seemed to me) for the future of law in our country. I knew one of the law reporters well. I would explain to him how important the case was. But when the argument reached its climax (by which I mean when I was eloquently defending the fundamental rights of my client and all mankind) the reporter always seemed to be away having his coffee.

'Nationalisation' (if that be the right expression—and it is not) of law reporting was not made total when the Incorporated Society of Law Reporting came into existence, any more than the National Health Act prevented the continuance of private medicine and pay-beds in hospitals. Private industry continued to flourish in the shape of several series of reports, for example:

(a) *The Times Law Reports* (TLR), but these ended in 1952.
(b) *The Law Times* (LT), which merged into the *All England Reports* in 1948.
(c) *The Law Journal Reports* (LJR), which joined forces with the *All England Reports* in 1950.
(d) The *All England Reports* (All ER) which began in 1936 and are of considerable importance. In their thin, closely types pages, there are a tremendous number of reports (far more than in the Law Reports); and they have the advantage—rare in legal books—of a very good index. They do not, however, include counsels' submissions.
(e) In 1947 *Current Law* (CL) began, making the extravagant claim of providing 'all the law from every source'. Because there is so much in it, and it is so condensed, it tends to be a rather indigestible publication; nevertheless the young advocate should consider taking out a subscription to it (it appears monthly). *Current Law* is particularly useful in providing carefully indexed guidance on quantum of damages in personal injury cases. A barrister's opinion on quantum that contains reference to a number of carefully selected cases from *Current Law* will often make a deep impression on the insurance company on the other side and ensure a favourable settlement. The practitioner dealing in accident cases cannot afford to be without *Current Law*, or *Kemp and Kemp on the Quantum of Damages*—of which more later.

The Times newspaper produces a law report, or law reports, almost daily, and although the judgments therein recorded are inevitably truncated so that reference must be made later to the full report if and when it appears, they have the distinction of being prompt, almost invariably accurate, and in no way slanted, which is more than can be said of many other newspaper reports. Other papers, like the *Guardian, Independent, Daily Telegraph* and *Financial Times,* have recently introduced their own law reports, and the *Financial Times* produces good reports of commercial cases. Legal practitioners should take *The Times*—for its law reports. My only complaint about them is the preponderance of space given to settled libel actions, which are of not the slightest importance to most members of the legal profession. Surely there are more vital matters to report from the courts.

Finally, when speaking of law reports in general, it would be wrong to omit those appearing in the *Justice of the Peace Newspaper* (JPN) covering as they do cases of sentencing in the Court of Appeal (Criminal Division), cases taken from magistrates' courts (and occasionally from Crown Courts) to the Divisional Court, and even more important to practitioners in the lower courts, controversial decisions reached in magistrates' courts. These reports are carefully selected for use by the practitioner in the magistrates' courts; they are set out in some detail, and do have persuasive authority.

Other reports that are of considerable use to the practitioner in criminal law are the excellent and succinct *Criminal Appeal Reports* (Cr App R or CAR), the *Criminal Law Review* (Crim LR) with its erudite commentaries and also *Cox's Criminal Cases* (Cox CC). These, like the Law Reports—and the *All England Reports*—must be edited by a barrister, and to this they owe their authenticity. Many other reports are not checked by the Bar and are therefore not automatically quotable in court, like those in the *Estates Gazette* (useful though these are for reference and guidance in landlord and tenant matters). The specialist in road traffic cases will have derived considerable comfort (since 1970) from the *Road Traffic Reports* (RTR), much commended by the judges. A new series on commercial cases came into existence recently for those practising in that esoteric—and lucrative—field (the *Commercial Law Reports*).

What do you do if you remember the name of a leading case but not its reference? You should be able to find it in the excellent index to the otherwise rather useless *English and Empire Digest*, which is now called 'the Digest', and from 1947 onwards it is almost certain to be in *Current*

Law. Alternatively, the index to the *Law Reports Digest* should be of assistance.

As I mentioned in an earlier chapter, the legal knowledge that you acquire from your research of the law reports is not your private and secret prerogative. The etiquette of your profession requires that you should spread it around. If there is an authority against you, you must show it to the other side (whose advocate may not have been as diligent as you, through no fault of his own, as he may not have had as much time for preparation). If the party on the other side is unrepresented, you must call the judge's attention to the adverse authority. Your skill as an advocate will be taxed to the full in trying to distinguish your case on its facts from the authority you have revealed, but at least the judge will be leaning over backwards to help you because of your honesty and devotion to the cause of justice. If this sounds like a counsel of perfection may I point out a possible effect of the opposite course of action (concealing the authority)? The judge is unaware of the authority. (Contrary to the popular belief among most young advocates, judges do not know everything—neither do most stipendiary magistrates.) You win your case. Shortly afterwards the litigant on the other side is consoling himself in a local hostelry. He confides to a group of people there the reasons for his sorrow. One of them is an articled clerk about to take his Solicitors' Finals (a most dangerous breed). He says: 'You ought never to have lost your action. The case of *Winkle* v *Snodgrass* is dead in your favour. Wasn't it mentioned?' On getting a negative answer he recommends the aggrieved litigant to come to see his principal with a view to appeal, and the latter persuades him that this is the correct course. In the fulness of time the matter comes before the Court of Appeal, and the Master of the Rolls has some biting comments to make about the inadequacies of the trial judge, and of your opponent, but also of you, for failing to call the judge's attention to the relevant authority. *Winkle* v *Snodgrass* is indeed in point, the appeal is allowed, and your client is ordered to pay the costs incurred in the Court of Appeal and in the court below.

Your client is not very pleased with you. Your solicitor does not brief you again.

When I was at the Bar my opponents frequently revealed to me authorities in my favour of which I was unaware, and I did likewise. In addition they (and I) would almost invariably reveal to the other side the authority on which we intended to rely so that they could prepare to argue against them. This is only fair: all too often a barrister has a case thrown at him at the last minute and has no time to go to the library. To this rule there was one exception in my professional life, which I regret (but not very much). At the end of the second chapter I mentioned how in my early days at the Bar I had a long 'fight' against an opponent who used almost every dirty trick in his very considerable repertoire, and who had earned for himself a generally unsavoury reputation (which he still enjoys). Some years later we were involved in a Rent Act dispute in the Shoreditch County Court in which he was appearing for two joint landlords and I was for the tenant. The issues were that the tenant should be compelled to give up possession of his home as the other side needed the premises for personal occupation, and greater hardship would be caused to the landlords by being kept out of the accommodation than by the tenant's having to surrender possession. One of the two landlords gave evidence and, if he were telling the truth, he had a strong case. The other landlord did not give evidence; he was living in Australia.

Now I had found an authority that said that where there were joint landlords both must satisfy the court that they or their families intended to live in the property if an order were to be made. Nothing was said on behalf of the distant landlord and his relations. So I had my authority with me. I thought, having read the particulars of claim, settled by solicitors, that the other side might be unaware of my authority and I went to court prepared to show it to my opponent—until I saw who it was. Then I contented myself with watching the expression on his face as I produced my authority from under the desk and submitted no case to answer. It was not the right thing to do, but I salved my conscience by assuring myself that it was exactly what he would have done to me or to any other advocate had the positions been reversed. A good reputation with your peers in the profession is a considerable asset.

If a young barrister who had just completed his pupillage came to me and asked me what qualities he should look for in his first set of Chambers I should advise three things: (1) a first-rate clerk; (2) congenial companions; and (3) a good library. A young solicitor looking for his first working 'home' would be advised to seek the same sort of advantages, *mutatis mutandis*. I don't know too well the situation of solicitors embarking on their professional career, although I believe it to be difficult, but so far as the barrister is concerned he would need a double first at Oxbridge and a Certificate of Honour in the Bar Finals before making such demands. It will therefore be more useful, perhaps, if I merely quote a few textbooks (a few, because law books, with their limited circulation, are very expensive) which the aspiring advocate should have for his own personal use, because he or she will so often need to refer to them in the course of, I hope, daily practice in the courts. In all cases except Bullen and Leake he should have the latest edition—nothing 'dates' as quickly as this living organism called 'the law'.

Of his student textbooks he should keep *Cross on Evidence* (Butterworths) and constantly familiarise himself with it. As I have indicated before, a working knowledge of the law of evidence is the most essential ingredient in the good advocate's armoury. He should also retain *Odgers on Pleading and Practice* (Sweet & Maxwell), which contains a few—all too few—useful precedents for pleading at the back. I once discovered a precedent in Odgers which was not to be found in *Atkins' Forms and Precedents* or in Bullen and Leake. I have already mentioned how useful that husband-and-wife work *Kemp and Kemp on the Quantum of Damages* (Sweet & Maxwell) will be to anyone who has to deal in the distressing realm of accident cases (which I sincerely hope will soon be replaced by 'No Fault' compensation, as in New Zealand—see the Pearson Report). If he has already acquired *Megarry on the Rent Acts* (Sweet & Maxwell) he should keep this too, for it will be very useful to him in many landlord and tenant cases in the county court. He or she will undoubtedly be doing a lot of motoring cases early on, and *Road Traffic Law* by Linda Dobbs and Mark Lucraft (published by Waterlow) is a useful and much more compact and economical modern alternative to the conventional *Wilkinson's Road Traffic Offences.*

If you are going to do criminal work you must have *Archbold's Criminal Pleading, Evidence and Practice* (Sweet & Maxwell), known as the criminal practitioner's 'Bible'. You can't do without it, especially as some of your more sophisticated clients will know the parts that affect their cases by heart and by paragraph. (Charles Richardson certainly did!) A few years ago *Archbold* was given a new format to which I have not yet wholly accustomed myself. Perhaps one day some keen young lawyer will get round to giving it an intelligible index! For the magistrates' courts you will need *Stone's Justices' Manual* (Butterworths) (equally weak on index) which, alas, comes out annually and runs to three volumes. If there are two or more copies in Chambers or the office you might be able to get by without actually purchasing it for a year or two. For criminal work in magistrates' courts *Brian Harris's Criminal Jurisdiction of Magistrates* (Kluwer) is an excellent guide—much cheaper than *Stone* and less heavy to cart around—but of course it does not cover family work. There used to be a rule that you could not refer to a textbook as authority until its author was dead, but happily that rule has never been applied since *Megarry*.

Unfortunately some of the books with which the student used to get by in the examinations must now be discarded in favour of weightier tomes. *Tolstoy on Divorce* will need to be replaced by *Rayden* (Butterworths)—a difficult book to understand, I always thought, but it contains good precedents for pleading family matters—or by *Latey*, a more readable textbook. However *Stone* will suffice, so long as the advocate confines his family work to the magistrates' courts. If his practice in landlord and tenant is likely to extend beyond the Rent Act cases for which he will find *Megarry* so useful, he must acquire *Woodfall* (Sweet &

Maxwell). The law on licensing (liquor and betting) is nebulous because decisions turn very much on the attitude and practice of licensing justices in particular areas. I recall an unavailing struggle on a meritorious application to get a betting office licence in an especially beautiful West Country town. The justices—and particularly their clerk (now a Crown Court judge) did not want the town spoiled by such an intrusion; I can understand their point of view; and it is far easier to get a new liquor licence in London than in Llangollen. But if you are likely to be caught up in the weird and wonderful world of licensing (and the law of liquor licensing is very complicated) you will certainly need the latest edition of *Paterson's Licensing Acts* (Butterworths)—another difficult book, but undoubtedly one to have. I wrote the first edition of this book in Suffolk, where I had been addressing Justices of the Peace. The clerk to the Lowestoft Justices told me that he believed that his predecessor, John Martin, had been editor of *Paterson* longer than any other editor in legal history. On reflection I am not sure about this. I remember Victor Wellings QC now President of the Lands Tribunal, beavering away with *Woodfall* when we shared a room in Chambers nearly forty years ago. He is the greatest living expert on landlord and tenant that I know, except for former Vice-Chancellor Megarry.

If you are going to do civil work and as a student you used for the law of contract that lovely book *Cheshire and Fifoot* (Butterworths), both of whom lectured to me, you must abandon their academic approach for the more practical, heavier and much less readable *Chitty* (Sweet & Maxwell). Likewise on tort forget sweet old Professor Winfield (who gave us all a sherry party on his eightieth birthday, saying modestly: 'We are all students. You are students. I'm a student. You're always a student in the law')—or Salmond, in favour of the practitioner's book, *Clerk and Lindsell* (Sweet & Maxwell).

If you expect to be doing civil work you must at least have access to the *Supreme Court Practice* (the *'White Book'*). Let's hope there is more than one copy in your Chambers or office because you will be needing it when you are rushed over to the law courts for a 1.30 Master's summons. But you may do more work in the county court in your early years, and for this you will need the latest *County Court Practice* (the '*Green Book*'). This you should buy as (a) it is cheaper than the White Book, and (b) you will have to take it much further away from your headquarters, and you will not be popular if it disappears from Chambers or the office. (I am no tax lawyer, but I imagine that any of these essential books that you buy for your practice can be set off against tax.)

Finally, as a civil lawyer—certainly if you are at the Bar—you must have a good book of precedents for your pleadings, and the best is undoubtedly *Bullen and Leake on Precedents of Pleadings* (Sweet & Maxwell). Here I can offer a word of comfort. Get as old an edition as possible, second-hand, just as cheaply as you can. The more modern it gets, the less good it seems. My own edition, which had a Victorian flavour (and odour) about it, contained references to plaintiffs being run down by horses and broughams, but with a little modernisation in keeping with the times it was capable of producing some eloquent pleadings. I think the judges liked them!

I have assumed throughout that the young advocate to whom this chapter is primarily addressed is almost as impecunious as I was when I started at the Bar. If I am mistaken about this, and my readership consists entirely of the legal descendants of Baron Rothschild, then I would recommend such people to acquire *Halsbury's Laws of England* and *Halsbury's Statutes*, each running to about forty costly volumes. If modesty or availability of space would preclude the reader's purchasing both sets, then my preference would be for the *Statutes*: I always found the notes thereto particularly useful. I was fortunate to find myself in a set of Chambers that had both the *Laws* and the *Statutes*. My 'double first' of earlier on should ensure that his potential Chambers are equally well endowed before accepting the offer of a tenancy! *Halsbury's Laws* has the advantage of having every legal topic in alphabetical order. It is the only attempt that has ever been made to set out the whole of English law in one voluminous document. As one who practised at the Bar for seventeen years I hope that my solicitor readers will not attach too much significance to the fact that the topic of 'barristers' falls between 'bankrupts' and 'bastards'.

I did eventually buy *Halsbury's Laws of England*—but not for myself, I hasten to add. In 1955 I was lecturing at the University of Leiden and Professor de Grooth, Professor of English Law there, asked me to try to get him a set for his University Library. I succeeded in finding one for sale by a barrister who was retiring. It cost, then, I think, £300. I sent it off, by boat to Holland. It arrived, less one volume. (I had failed to insure the package.) The international repercussions of this were enormous, and extremely worrying. I can only hope that the British or Dutch docker who took the volume to add to his library has enjoyed his 'light' reading.

12 The advocate's duty to the court

Many years ago Lord Atkin said:

> 'The code of honour of the legal profession is at once its most cherished possession and the most valued safeguard of the public. In the discharge of his office the advocate has a duty to his client, a duty to his opponent, a duty to the Court, a duty to the State, and a duty to himself. To maintain a perfect poise amidst the various and sometimes conflicting claims is no easy task.'

I like to think that those words are still true today.

So far as the advocate's duty to the court is concerned, he must never knowingly be a party to the deception of the court, either by asserting something that he knows or believes to be untrue or by deliberately suppressing information that he knows to be germane to the matter in issue. As indicated elsewhere, however—and the authority for this is no less than that of Lord Goddard—he need not, after conviction, reveal other convictions of which the prosecution seems unaware. There is no reason why a defendant should be in a worse position through having instructed an advocate than if he chose to represent himself, and no sane defendant, hearing the prosecutor on conviction or plea of guilty say 'Nothing known', would chirp up with: 'Oh yes there is. I'm really a person of bad character'. A Crown Court judge complained to me the other day: 'I had to send to prison a chap I didn't want to put inside at all. When the police officer gave out his list of previous convictions I saw no need to imprison the defendant, but then his idiot counsel told me that he was subject to a six months suspended sentence, so now he's doing seven months.' A gloss on this must be presented in the light of the proceedings brought late in 1987 against a solicitor named John Francis Bridgwood both in the criminal courts and before the Law Society's Disciplinary Committee. I take the facts of the matter from the *Law Society's Gazette* of 5 July 1989:

> 'Mr Bridgwood was contacted by a client for whom he had acted on many previous occasions. The client was facing criminal charges at Manchester City Magistrates' Court. The client told Mr Bridgwood that she had given the police a false name and address and date of birth and Mr Bridgwood advised her to reveal her true identity to the police as it would be established in any event through fingerprint evidence. Some two weeks later Mr Bridgwood attended court where he was contacted again by his client. He discovered that the prosecution had not established his client's true identity. He was able to spend only a very short period of time with his client prior to the case being called into the court and his client's instructions to him were that she intended to appear before the court using the false name. Mr Bridgwood went into court with his client who pleaded guilty in her false name and Mr Bridgwood spoke in mitigation. He considered that he could act properly on her behalf provided he did not refer to her assumed name and provided that he had made no reference to her character.
>
> In November 1987 Mr Bridgwood was tried and convicted in the Crown Court on a charge of acting in a manner tending and intending to pervert the course of public justice. He was sentenced to nine months' imprisonment, suspended for two years. He was subsequently fined £2,000 by the Solicitors' Disciplinary Tribunal.'

In the light of those two decisions in the *Bridgwood* case I think that Lord Goddard's advice must now be modified, and I cannot think that the Bar would wish to apply standards any less rigorous than those imposed by the Law Society. The facts of the *Bridgwood* case are somewhat exceptional, but I think that, since the introduction of the Crown Prosecution Service, the information given to the court about a defendant's previous convictions is often inaccurate: I would not be at all surprised if it were seriously wrong in more than 50 per cent of cases. A lot of defendants whom I have recognised as 'regulars' have been presented to the court by the CPS as people of previous good character. In many other cases records have been lost or incomplete, and, most significantly, suspended sentences to which the defendant has been subject have not been included on the Criminal Records Office form. This is presented to the defending advocate, who is asked if he 'accepts' it. His client has told him that his main worry is that he is subject to a suspended sentence, but this does not appear on the form. What is the defending advocate to do? He has a duty to be frank and honest with the court but also a duty to secure the best possible outcome for his client, certainly one no worse than would ensue were the defendant unrepresented. This is the wise advice given by the Law Society in this all too common situation: 'It is advised that in future solicitors . . . should decline to comment on the accuracy of such lists.'

The line taken by many good solicitors at my last court (Horseferry Road) was, when asked to endorse the accuracy of the Criminal Records Office forms, to comment: 'I have no observations to make'. In order to avoid letting down their more regular and reliable clients by a process of elimination they did this both in the cases where the CRO form was accurate (the minority of cases, I suspect) and where they knew it to be inaccurate. This is an approach which I commend to the Bar as well as to solicitors until such time as the police and the CPS can get their act together. However, reports of decisions against you of which you are aware must be revealed, both to the court and to the other side, as stated in the previous chapter. Your skill must then be deployed in seeking to distinguish such cases from the instant one.

But your duty to the court extends further than this. You should try, whichever side you are on, to help the court in its difficult task of reaching a just decision. This involves careful preparation. You have the opportunity of knowing all about the case before it comes to court. The judge or magistrates, unlike their continental counterparts, have not. If it is a personal injury action, be sure to have available decisions indicating the current range of damages in similar cases: the judge may not have had experience of a case like yours before.

In the criminal courts, do your best to expedite matters by making sure that your client's plea, as entered by him, is unambiguous and quite unequivocal. In magistrates' courts a great deal of time is wasted by the plea of 'Guilty, but . . .' This is understandable in the case of an unrepresented defendant, unforgivable when the defendant has an advocate present. I have now recovered from the attack of apoplexy from which I suffered when an advocate said to me in a shop-lifting case: 'I ask you to give him credit for pleading guilty, Your Worship, and he instructs me to say that he is very sorry that he did not pay for these goods as he was very drunk at the time'.

The tasks in which the judges and magistrates seek and are entitled to seek your help is not, I assure you, an easy one. In the magistrates' courts the most difficult aspect of the work relates to decisions regarding bail and sentence. Those appearing before the court tend to be divided into three categories: the bad, the sad, and the mad.

When I started sitting as a magistrate there were basically only six decisions available to the court:

(i) absolute discharge, reserved then (as now) for the purely technical offence to which no moral blame attaches;
(ii) conditional discharge, then for up to one year as a maximum;
(iii) probation, for between one year and three years;
(iv) a fine, of up to £100;
(v) immediate imprisonment for up to six months; or
(vi) detention centre for three to six months for young offenders under twenty-one.

The law relating to compensation in criminal cases was so complex then that magistrates' courts usually chose to ignore it.

Since 1967 the law relating to all these headings has changed, and compensation is readily available to the victims of almost all criminal acts except those arising from motor vehicle accidents. In addition, the armoury of the sentencer has been extended enormously with the introduction of the suspended sentence, the partly suspended sentence, youth custody, the deferred sentence, heavier fines, attendance centres, community service orders, and day training centres—and I am sure that I have not exhausted the list. All this is to the good. The greater the options open to the court, the greater the chance of its doing justice, but the advocate must be prepared to remind the court of what seems most appropriate in his particular case. The suggestion put forward must be realistic. I was not very favourably impressed by the concluding sentence from the report of a probation officer on a young burglar whom I had to sentence:

> 'As he has not paid any of his fines, and he did not turn up for his community service assessment, and his probation had to be terminated because of his failure to keep appointments, and he is already the subject of a suspended sentence, I can only suggest a conditional discharge in this case.' (I did find another solution.)

Nor was I greatly assisted by the report of a psychiatrist (which I retain and treasure because of its novelty, and which I have before me now) on a young man of nineteen with a variety of criminal offences to his discredit, who had taken a car without the consent of the owner, driven it while disqualified and while drunk, driven at speeds exceeding 80 mph through the streets of West London in the middle of the night, driven the wrong way up one-way streets and on the wrong side of a dual carriageway, finally crashed into three other vehicles which, along with the one he was driving, he had wrecked, and then tried to run away from the scene until he had collapsed in a drunken heap. I leave the reader to work out how many sections of the Road Traffic Acts he had breached!

I quote from the psychiatrist's report:

> 'I felt him to be a boy suffering from the sequelae of emotional privation in earlier years . . . For two weeks before committing these offences he was living with his mother, who repeatedly exalted [*sic*] him as to what he should and what he should not do as though he were a very young child. Though he did not protest to his mother, a feature of certain of the offences which followed (particularly his driving on the wrong side of a dual carriageway and the wrong way up one-way streets) appears to be a protest against all the restrictions of his mother . . .
>
> He has, in my opinion, now lived for too long independently of parental authority, or of authority resembling that of a parent, to be willing to submit to such now. I therefore wish to recommend that the court treat this case by means of a probation order, which I believe would prove to be of value.'

I told the defendant, as I sent him in custody on his way to the Crown Court to meet Judge Friend: 'You know, I'm not a clever psychiatrist, but I have a feeling that when you were driving at 80 mph the wrong way up one-way streets and on the wrong side of the dual carriageway, you weren't thinking of your mother at all. I believe you were looking in the mirror of the car you had taken and you saw the police car chasing after you.'

There was a suggestion a few years ago that judges and magistrates should be replaced by sentencing panels comprising probation officers, psychiatrists and teachers, who are thought to be more 'in touch' with defendants than the Judiciary. The proposed scheme had its attractions for me: early retirement and redundancy pay were among them. But when I contemplated it more deeply, I thought of that probation officer's report and that psychiatrist's report . . .

So try to do better than they, please! And in all that you do, be pleasant and good-humoured. While I was writing the first edition, young counsel came before me on the committal of a very well-dressed young man (also nineteen) charged with stealing ladies' handbags from a club. He asked to get on early, as he had to rush away to another court, and we facilitated this. The defendant had failed to appear to answer to his bail the previous week. As the formalities of the committal were being conducted by the clerk of the court, I followed my usual custom of looking through the prosecution statements to try to assess the strength or weakness of the case against the defendant. I saw that the young man (who was in full employment) had hired a taxi to go to the club, requested the taxi-driver to wait for a few minutes, and then had emerged from the club with the ladies' bags and that the taxi-driver had been instrumental in securing his arrest. My browsing was interrupted by counsel who said, sharply: 'I hope you are not thinking of withholding bail in this case'. I told him that it had crossed my mind. When I learned from the police officer that the defendant had two previous convictions for very similar offences earlier that year this, combined with his 'forgetting' to come to court the previous week, convinced me that to withhold bail would be the right thing to do. Counsel made his disagreement with me very clear. I did not hear the comment that he made to the others in counsels' bench, but I do not think somehow that it was very complimentary, as he threw his brief down angrily on the table before him, then picked it up and flounced out of the door which he slammed loudly. He was so angry that he forgot to ask for an extension of the legal aid certificate, an omission which, knowing his instructing solicitor, I feel will have caused grave disquiet in that particular quarter.

Don't be a temperamental prima donna. Bad temper and histrionics towards the Bench are as inappropriate as they are on the Bench.

The worst example of rudeness to which I have been subjected in court came in what used to be called a 'sus' case (being a suspected person loitering with intent to commit an arrestable offence). The judicial proceedings in that case being over, I think I can properly write about it, as it is a good example of how an advocate should NOT behave in court.

Contrary, I am sure to the view of the solicitor concerned, Neville Kesselman, I was against the archaic 'sus' law. It always seemed to me too vague in its essence, the wording of the charge contained an implication of guilt, and it deprived the defendant of his right of trial by jury in cases which, in reality, often amounted to attempted theft. I campaigned against 'sus' and was glad when it was removed from the statute book. Even so, while it was still the law, I think that occasionally people did try car doors with the intention of taking the car or removing something from it.

That was the allegation in this particular case. When the defendant was arrested, 'sus' was still part of the law. So it was when he should have appeared before me. But he chose not to come to court. (Later he was to plead guilty before me to an offence against s 6(1) of the Bail Act 1976). By the time he was arrested and brought before me for trial, 'sus' was no longer law, having been replaced by the Criminal Attempts Act 1981.

The solicitor began by making an able, forceful and succinct submission that I now had no jurisdiction to try the case. I ruled against him, and directed that the trial should proceed. The first of two police officers gave evidence. (We were never to get beyond his evidence.) He gave an account of the defendant's suspicious activities. The solicitor rose to cross-examine. The young officer was subjected to the longest, most vigorous, most unpleasant cross-examination that I have ever heard in a magistrates court. It finished (at least, I presume this was intended to be the final onslaught) with this comment in the guise of a question:

'I put it to you, officer, that the whole of your evidence in this case is a carbon copy of what you have been taught at Hendon Police College in your efforts to get down the blacks.' (According to the police officer, the solicitor had also spat at him, but I did not see this happen although two other persons in court did.)

It was at this point that I intervened for the first time

to say to the solicitor: 'You do not often come to my Court, I am glad to say, so you may not be accustomed to our ways. We have a tradition here of courtesy—courtesy to advocates, courtesy to defendants, courtesy to witnesses, courtesy even to police officers. I am afraid you have fallen below our standards.'

Mr Kesselman replied: 'I am sorry if I have had to be aggressive, but it would not have been necessary if you had not reached such a stupid decision at the beginning of the case'.

At that point I must confess that I broke my own rule and lost my temper. 'If my ruling was so stupid', I said, 'go and test it in the Divisional Court. I refuse to hear any more of this today' and I fixed a date for the resumed hearing, giving the defendant unconditional bail.

He did take it to the Divisional Court, and won! That court issued a writ of prohibition to prevent me from resuming the hearing. The prosecution felt aggrieved. There were hundreds of cases similar to this one in the pipeline, and the principle affected thousands of other more serious cases pending or which might be pending on a change of the law and they were going to seek leave to appeal to the House of Lords (but had not yet done so). On the day to which I had adjourned the case both sides came back to me, the prosecution—now represented for the first time before me—to ask me further to adjourn it, Mr Kesselman to ask me to dismiss it. His argument included what sounded like a threat: 'I warn you of the direst consequences for you personally if you do not accede to my submission'. I did not find this way of presenting his case very attractive, and I ruled against him. But he had meant what he said! A few days later I was served with a writ seeking to commit me to prison for contempt of court. In the meantime my wife had received an intimidating telephone call from him at our home.

On our days off we are 'on call' lest another stipendiary magistrate should fall sick. This happened shortly after I received my writ and I was asked to go to sit at Old Street. There was a bus that went most of the way there from my home and I decided to take it. It moved slowly and I got restive and kept worrying the bus conductress as to when we might reach the court. She was a kindly woman and patient with me, but when I got off she remarked: 'I hope they won't put you inside, sir'. Believing that she had mistaken me for a defendant on bail I corrected her: 'No, no, nobody's going to put me inside today'. She repeated, just as I got off the bus outside the court: 'No, I hope they don't send you to prison, Mr Crowther'.

I pondered this extraordinary conversation much of the day. The solution was to reach me that evening, when a friend of mine, who was both a Member of Parliament and a barrister, told me that the previous evening there had been a television programme in which it seems that the solicitor who had employed Mr Kesselman as agent (although they are both in London he preferred to engage the services of another solicitor rather than counsel) had been arguing to so many of the great British public as choose to watch BBC2 the merits of my being sent to gaol on account of my 'considering myself above the law', with my picture in the corner of the screen. Neither of the two solicitors concerned, nor the BBC had had the courtesy to advise me about the programme, and the BBC has ignored my requests to see it subsequently. My friend, however, described the programme as 'disgraceful', and I think that it is carrying enthusiasm for one's case—in general a commendable quality—too far.

So did Ackner LJ when the application to commit me to prison was heard. He described it as 'the height of absurdity' and 'wholly devoid of any merit'. I remained at liberty.

In duty course, as it happened, the House of Lords upheld my decision to continue to hear the case. The defendant pleaded guilty to the Bail Act matter and then I learned that he was subject to a conditional discharge—for 'sus'—I ordered him to pay a fine for the Bail Act offence and legal aid costs. He still has not done so.

It would seem, however, that the conduct of the solicitors concerned was not unbefitting to their profession. It may come as no surprise that as soon as the matter ended in August 1982 I complained to the Law Society. They obviously considered the matter seriously: it took them eighteen months to reach a decision. Little wonder, then perhaps, that an ordinary citizen named Mr Parsons felt sufficiently dissatisfied with their procedure to go to the High Court about it—see *In re a Solicitor* (1983) *The Times*, 19 October and the *Law Society's Gazette* of 23 November 1983. But the Law Society's conclusion in my case may surprise the reader. It was conveyed to me in February 1984, by no lesser a personage then the Chairman of the Professional Purposes Committee. I will quote from his eventual lengthy reply to my complaints:

> 'It is difficult to establish whether the solicitor went beyond the bounds of his duty to his client . . . There is nothing inherently unprofessional in his having communicated with your wife . . . My Committee did not consider there was unbefitting conduct . . .
>
> It is clear that the solicitor appeared on BBC television with his client's consent. In the view of my Committee, provided that there was no contempt of court, he was entitled to do so . . .
>
> The Society can only take action where there is sufficient evidence to establish unbefitting conduct . .
>
> My Committee did not consider that there was sufficient evidence to enable them to take any action in respect of your complaint.'

Since then the Law Society has been pressing the solicitors to be allowed to extend their right of audience in the Crown Court, and to be permitted to appear in all courts, and this may well be sanctioned under the Courts and Legal Services Bill. I regret that (despite the admiration that I feel for most of the excellent solicitors who have appeared before me) I cannot support them in this respect.

In an earlier chapter I quoted Lord Dunboyne, in an address which he gave to overseas students at the British Council Student Centre. 'Paddy', as he is affectionately called, is well known for his generosity both with his time and in other respects to students and to young people, and when I was an advocate I always found him, as a judge, courteous and pleasant to appear before. It was therefore with some dismay that I read in *The Times* of remarks made by counsel in his closing address to the jury—remarks so offensive towards the judge that I do not propose to give them further currency by repeating them here—which caused Lord Dunboyne to reply: 'There is a disastrous undercurrent which is beginning to pervade parts of the Bar: barristers trying to score points off the judge, with blazing rows if possible, either with a view to appeal or by currying points with the jury—this is highly undesirable . . . and a disgrace to the Bar'.

Such conduct is quite inexcusable. There can be only two reasons for it: to achieve publicity through notoriety; and to make an impression on one's clients. I can only say that the sort of clients who are impressed by that kind of behaviour are not worth cultivating; they are the sort who will afford the advocate little joy and endless trouble.

Now that the trial of David Martin is over, and he has committed suicide at the beginning of a sentence of 25 years' imprisonment, having faced numerous charges including attempting to murder a policeman and escaping from the cells at Marlborough Street Court on Christmas Eve 1982, and now that the case of the two policemen who were accused of attempting to murder Stephen Waldorf (whom they mistook for Martin) is also over and they have been acquitted, I can comment on the conduct of the solicitor who appeared for Mr Martin.

An article that began on the front page of the *Evening Standard* on 31 January 1982 reads as follows:

> 'Outside Marlborough Street Court, the defendant's solicitor spoke to reporters and read a statement which he had taken down after talking to Martin. [It included the following passages:]
>
> He (David Martin) considers he is greatly indebted to Steven Waldorf whom he has never met. But for what happened to Mr Waldorf, Mr Martin is convinced he would have been shot in the course of his arrest . . .
>
> He says that he won't eat or drink, at least until he is allowed to see (his girlfriend).' [The last prediction, incidentally, proved to be untrue.]

On the face of it, it seems to me that such a statement, if the newspaper report be accurate, could be construed as a contempt of the court that was ultimately to try David Martin; a contempt of the court that was to try the two police officers, and a gross contempt of the court from which that experienced solicitor—for whom up to then I had had great admiration—had just emerged, presided over by St John Harmsworth, then one of London's senior and most distinguished stipendiary magistrates. I repeat here, in part, what appears to have been said in the hope that no solicitor or barrister will ever seek to emulate such conduct. The advocate is a filter, not a mouthpiece or a publicity agent. It did the solicitor no good at all. Subsequently, David Martin dismissed him and appointed the solicitor who was to act for him at his trial at the Old Bailey.

Not all the difficulties that are incurred in judicial office arise from the attitude of advocates. Quite often it is the ambivalence of Parliament that is to blame. In the chapter on bail I referred to the anguish that I suffered because of an anomaly in the Bail Act depriving me, as it seemed, from denying bail to a man whose main intent at liberty was to murder. Other recent pronouncements of Parliament give rise to further problems. It came as something of a surprise to me to realise that a young man, charged under the Trading Representation (Disabled Persons) Act with pretending (very convincingly, judging by his 'credentials') to be collecting money for the severely handicapped, could not be sentenced to imprisonment in a magistrates' court (and so could not be ordered to do Community Service, which might have been appropriate). The worst thing that could happen to him was a fine, and, as his very lucrative source of income, which he had enjoyed for quite a long time, had now been terminated on account of the inconsiderate activity of the police in apprehending him, so that he was now on minimal social security, there was, in truth, nothing realistic that I could do with him.

In order to reduce the prison population the Home Secretary has decided that vagrants and beggars and prostitutes can no longer be imprisoned. This is a source of some disappointment to certain members of the first two groups, though certainly not to the last. But the maximum fines on beggars and vagrants have been substantially increased! In the case of some young beggars who need money to satisfy their craving for hard drugs (especially heroin) the borderline between begging and attempted robbery is a little difficult to discern. I was once invited to a party down the Earls Court Road. (I do not frequently walk in that particular area: I have too many acquaintances there. However, I chose to do so on this particular night.) As I walked down that notorious street a young man with glaring eyes approached me and asked me the time. Assuming that the watch that he was wearing had stopped I looked at my own chronometer and as I did so I realised that I was being edged into a corner. Suddenly, with his direct gaze upon me, he said: 'Give me some bread, man. I need 50 pence. Give it to me'. I put my hands in my pockets and pulled them out and showed them to be devoid of coinage. The man who appeared to have mistaken me for a baker became upset and shouted: 'You got to give me bread, man. I need bread', and he raised his fists towards my chin. It was then that I had an idea. 'I'm sorry that I'm unable to help you', I said, 'but I know some people up the road who may perhaps lend you 50 pence. Come along with me.' This seemed to mollify him, and we walked up Earls Court Road together in silence, but as we approached Kensingon Police Station he ran off. But had he been arrested, and charged with begging, all that my colleague Jimmy Cook could have done with him was fine him—and presumably he did not have even 50 pence.

Now I turn to the problems created by the change in the law relating to prostitutes. Many people write to me advising me what to do. In some cases what they suggest appears physically impossible; in others the adoption of their recommendations would result in a vacancy in the ranks of the Metropolitan Magistracy. But now it is I who am seeking advice. What is to be done with the prostitutes? Ignoring the obvous answer, may I explain the dilemma in a little more detail?

Imprisonment for prostitution was abolished in February

1983. Prior to that a prostitute could not be imprisoned before her third such conviction, and it must be remembered that discharges (absolute and conditional) and orders of probation do not qualify as convictions. Allowing for the fact that the girl would usually have been cautioned before being prosecuted, that she would probably have been the subject of conditional discharges (though rarely of probation), she would 'have come to the notice of police' for this offence many times before imprisonment was even contemplated. Before imposing even a suspended sentence of imprisonment the court would have had to offer her, on legal aid, the services of an advocate to persuade it that such a draconian measure was unnecessary, and she was likely to be committed to prison (for some period between five days and three months) only if she solicited again while the subject of the suspended sentence. Even so, the sanction of imprisonment at the end of the road (or street) did seem to act as a deterrent. There are a lot more prostitutes to be seen in London and other big cities today (or rather tonight) than they were a year or two ago.

With imprisonment gone, what alternatives remain? An absolute discharge should be reserved for a purely technical offence involving no moral turpitude; a conditional discharge will be ineffective because it will have no bite—there will be no motive not to re-offend; probation for prostitutes has never been popular with probation officers (whose views merit consideration) because they say it hardly ever works and so is a waste of their time.

Community service? 'I've done enough of that already, dear', remarked one such girl to whom this proposition was put; and in any event community service is available only in respect of offences carrying imprisonment (Powers of Criminal Courts Act 1973, s 14).

So, what remains? The darling of the Home Office (which ignores the fact that so many go uncollected, that so much police and court time is wasted in trying to collect those that are unpaid for months and years): fines, bigger and better fines. 'Time to pay, sir', asks the girl brightly. 'How long do you need to go and earn the money?' enquires the magistrate solicitously, 'Twenty minutes', was the surprising reply of one girl as she looked anxiously at her watch. But is it really desirable that he should be an accessory to the next offence, by 'counselling and procuring' that it should be committed within the time that the court sets? That is our problem. How are we able realistically to deal with this type of offence without ourselves seeming to encourage it?

There is a more serious aspect to all this. The London prostitute of today is no longer the blasé blowsy woman of a quarter of a century ago. In my court she was usually seventeen or eighteen, still quite immature, from the provinces or the country, and attracted to London by the rumour that all the Arabs around were swimming in oil and swathed in gold. My colleagues in the juvenile courts tell me that they are getting much younger girls, who have run away from home, appearing before them for this offence. Once I had before me a nineteen year old girl, of excellent family, who lived a couple of streets away from me. Lazy by nature, she found the life easy, pleasurable and profitable. She did not realise for quite a long time the fact that she was being watched by a special kind of man (perhaps the one frequently to be seen in the public gallery when a new girl appears, who leaves as soon as she has been dealt with—one learns almost as much by studying the people in the public gallery as by looking at the defendant in the dock). Eventually he makes his approach to her. He is courteous and suave, and I imagine it goes someting like this:

'Now you seem to me to be a sensible business girl and I've got a business proposition to put to you. I've heard what you do. It can't be very nice always going back to the man's flat or hotel room. You never know what he may do to you there. Why don't I get you a place of your own for this? You'll feel safe there. You'll be in command. I'll pay the rent and all the expenses. You give me 25 per cent of what you earn and keep the rest. You'll be far better off in the long run. Think it over.'

She does, and decides in favour. It sounds fair enough, giving her more independence. The man seems to treat her fairly, takes her out on her 'nights off', becomes her friend —perhaps the only person she can really regard as a friend. It is when he has gained her confidence completely, when she feels a bit in love with him (for prostitutes have real feelings for some people—usually not their clients) that, perhaps one night when he has given her too much to drink, he introduces her to drugs: soft drugs and amphetamines at first, then 'something that will make you feel on top of the world'. It is only when he injects her with heroin for the first time that she is really lost. From then on she will work for her supply of dope, the price of which will get higher and higher, and it will be withheld unless she works harder and harder. And this situation will continue until she is unfit for more work and left to die; and the man looks for another little shrimp from Sheffield or Sutton Coldfield to fill the gap.

I am convinced that this does happen. I have read of it in a few probation reports (for the probation service do co-operate in providing reports in some of these cases) and from the deterioration that I have seen in the health of some of these girls as they have appeared frequently before me. You cannot sit as a magistrate for two decades without recognising the signs of injection of hard drugs. Up to February 1983 my method of dealing with these cases, where the young girl was not a Londoner (it was much more difficult when they did come from the capital), was to remand for four weeks for a probation report with a condition of bail that they went back now to live with Mum and reported to the probation officer in Manchester or Macclesfield first thing next morning, and stayed in their home town until the hearing (which I usually fixed for 2 pm so that they would not have to spend a night in London). Mum was usually thankful for the return of the prodigal daughter (of whose whereabouts and way of life she may have been unaware) and, with the co-operation of the probation service, the vicious circle was broken before it had even been formed, and in some cases broken for ever. Of course, the girls were warned that if they did not comply with the terms and conditions of bail they would go into custody for the preparation of the report, and this usually seemed to get them away from the scene of their activities, and the man lurking in the back of the court.

I was never quite sure if I were entitled to make this condition of bail in the case of a newcomer to the game, bearing in mind that although the offence of prostitution was prisonable she would not yet be liable to imprisonment; but fortunately no well-wisher of the professions (legal or oldest) ever took this crucial matter to the Divisional Court, and it is now too late to do so. Now that prostitution is no longer imprisonable there can be no doubt at all that questions of bail fall to be determined under the Second Schedule to the Bail Act 1976, and the imposition of conditions of bail such as those mentioned in the last preceding paragraph are highly dubious (but see the *Bournemouth Justices* case, (1989) JP 578), so the girls must probably be left to their (or their ponces') fate. Some magistrates say that this is a good thing. The courts are not, they say, agencies of social welfare. If that is so, why are we remanding for social enquiry reports, and helping people by placing them on probation, and awarding compensation and making presentations from the Poor Box?

But the answer appears to be that we should not care (for I am sure that few courts have ever imprisoned for prostitution except from motives of caring). But shall we care when the streets of London are once again as crowded with prostitutes as they were just before the Street Offences Act 1959 (except that now the prostitutes, like the policeman who bring them before us, will seem—and be—younger)? This I predict will happen. And if we are wrong to care, and should not do anything with these young girls except blithely fine them without bothering how they are to find the money to pay the fines, would it not be better if Parliament put a stop to this piece of hypocrisy by simply removing for all time from the Statute Book the offence of 'being a common prostitute'—a deplorable expression anyway—'soliciting for the purpose of prostitution'?

These are matters on which I should welcome advice.

13 The Crown Prosecution Service

For thirty years I helped to run the British Council Student Centre, which looked after the welfare of an average of 4,000 overseas students a year, until in 1981 the Council decided to close it down and transfer the funds hitherto expended on it to 'more cultural' activities. An overseas student once asked me: 'How many people actually work in the British Council?' Misunderstanding the question I replied 'About half of them'. I am not sure if the same answer could properly be given concerning the Crown Prosecution Service, but the quality of the service provided to the courts appears to vary between the excellent and the execrable.

On my last day of sitting as a magistrate, 22 September 1989, the Crown Prosecutor of the day, an Indian girl, concluded her duties by wishing me well in my retirement, and adding: 'You have sometimes been a severe critic of the CPS, but you have always been fair to us, and we have taken on board what you have said.' Well, I was never severely critical of her, because I had always found her competent, conscientious and intellectually honest. I would not apply those epithets to all her colleagues; one was accurately described, I thought, by one of my brother magistrates, as 'the archetypal wimp'. When I threw out a murder case against four Southern Irishmen who had for a long time been held in custody, remand after remand having been acceded to, I was strongly critical of a service which, in a matter as serious as murder, could lose the papers. Death had resulted from a single stab wound; only one weapon was involved, so it was likely that three of the people in the dock would be acquitted anyway. Nevertheless, the then Director, of Public Prosecutions (not Allan Green QC the present excellent Director, who came from the practising Bar) wrote me a very pained letter complaining of my 'unhelpful' remarks regarding a service which was in its infancy and was having 'teething troubles'. I am afraid that my reaction to that was that if one's teeth are as defective as those of the CPS at that time, it may be a case for total extraction. Others have been harsher in their comments on the service, especially in a debate in the House of Commons in February 1990.

But the failings of the CPS are in large measure the fault of the government, which introduced the measure far too quickly and with insufficient funding. In a society that has been encouraged to be mercenary, how could the government expect to attract people of high calibre by offering ridiculously low salaries? And having introduced a pilot scheme at a few courts (including my own at Horseferry Road) which produced chaos and disaster, why did they not consult with me and other magistrates before implementing the full scheme? In London it was grossly understaffed. Realising this, ultimately, the government raised salaries to a level so high that clerks in the Court Service were enticed away, and so now we have a shortage of court clerks and inefficiency on that count.

But one thing that the previous Director of Public Prosecutions emphasised when writing to me was that the Crown Prosecution Service is here to stay and we must make the best of it. The object of this chapter is to make recommendations as to how the service offered to the courts can be made better, and indeed I did notice a substantial improvement in standards in my last few months on the Bench. One has, moreover, to sympathise with the young man or woman who comes into court with fifty or sixty cases to handle in a morning or afternoon, with many defence counsel trying to get at the prosecutor with suggestions for compromise (no plea bargaining, of course!) or dates for adjournment.

Many years ago when I was at the Bar an Epsom solicitor who wanted to go to Ascot asked my clerk if I would do his 'list' in the Epsom County Court on Derby Day. (Judging by what he said afterwards regarding his success on the racecourse I think that he would have done better to attend the county court.) I had to deal with about a dozen matters varying from judgment summonses to possession actions and by the end of the proceedings I, who had never previously handled more than four cases in a day, felt, in the words of a colleague from a quieter court who once took over from me in a very busy one, 'whacked, absolutely whacked'.

But your Crown Prosecutor in a busy London court has to multiply my Epsom workload by four or five, and it is no easy task. So far as I can gather from observation, in London the CPS representative will appear in court only one half-day a week, usually in the morning, whereas in the afternoon one will usually have an agent, either solicitor or barrister, again varying from the intelligent to the unintelligible.

So the Crown Prosecution Service is here to stay. It is an important and valuable service which can be recommended to the newly qualified barrister or solicitor provided that he or she is prepared to work hard and is dedicated to the cause of justice. He must not, for example, throw in the sponge when a shoplifter elects to go for trial, on the ground that to go on would not be 'cost effective'. This is happening now, I understand, and when the news gets around all professional shoplifters will gain immunity by going for trial.

I am convinced, as are many who have spoken and written on the subject, that not all the defects in the presentation of cases are the fault of the Service. Many police officers regard the CPS with a mixture of envy and contempt: envy, because it is more comfortable to be in a nice warm court than on the beat, and contempt because they do not feel that the CPS is doing as good a job as they used to do when they prosecuted. All too often the reason given to the court for a trial not being able to go ahead is that 'the papers have not yet been received from the police'. Sometimes this is due to their not having been typed yet. The Metropolitan Police seem to employ the slowest typists in the country, while some defendants are languishing in custody. Not being conversant with what goes on behind the scenes before a case comes for trial I make a few suggestions for ameliorating this situation without being certain of how practical they are:

(1) Within a week of the arrest of any person on a serious charge—that term might have to be re-defined as not all 'either way' offences are really serious, although solely indictable offences obviously are—the matter shall be assigned to one person who shall have charge of preparing the case and presenting it in court. This would avoid the situation that we hear so often at present. 'This case has been handled by one of my colleagues but there is nothing in the papers to indicate who . . .'.

(2) Also within a week of the arrest there should be a meeting between that CPS representative and the police officer in charge of the case—or if he is 'on leave', as they so often seem to be, with one of the officers—when statements can be gone through and progress monitored so that a report can be made to the court at an early stage of the proceedings. The meeting of these two might convince each that the other was human and that there was a job to be done in unison.

(3) The restoration to all courts of a 'Court Inspector', or at least a sergeant deputising for him, sitting in court throughout the proceedings. In the days before the CPS, when these formidable figures were around, a policeman or a detective had only to get a rebuke from the court for one to see him being taken aside by his superior to receive a 'wigging' far worse than that inflicted by the Bench, and you could be sure that that officer would not let down the court again. Now, knowing that no-one of their own profession is going to record a black mark against them, some policemen and detectives are quite blatant in their indifference to criticisms emanating from the Bench.

But the main purpose of this chapter is to assist the young advocate who either decides on a career in the Crown Prosecution Service or who finds himself or herself lumbered with a file of papers to go and act as the Service's agent. Why are some prosecuting advocates so much more attractive, persuasive and convincing than others? Why does one heave a sigh of relief on entering into a magistrates' court on some days and simply heave a sigh on others? The answer is to be found in Chapter 2 on 'Preparation'.

If you know that you are going to have to present a heavy list next day, do not go out the night before. You are almost sure to have been given some papers: take them home and work on them! Make up a chart giving name(s) of defendants, age (it is very important when it comes to sentencing for the court to know if the defendant has attained the age of twenty-one, before which he can rarely be really effectively punished, however bad he is), the charge(s) he faces, a tick if he is of previous good character, and a note on your attitude to bail should there have to be a remand. Have immediately available at the front of the file dates on which witnesses will not be available and also the Criminal Record Office form showing the defendant's previous convictions, if this has been provided. If it has not (as is all too often the case) early arrival at court will enable you to ensure that this important information reaches the court in time, rather than having to ask for the case to be put back while these vital facts, so necessary for decisions on bail and sentencing, are obtained.

In seeking to establish why some Crown Prosecutors are so good while others are so bad I have sought advice from the fountain of all forensic knowledge, the gaolers, and they have provided the solution: the best are those who arrive at the court at 8.30; the worst those who stagger in with their piles of briefs just before the court begins. There have even been a few occasions in our busy Court No 1 when the usher has come to me around 10.35 to say: 'Sorry for the delay, but the Crown Prosecutor hasn't yet arrived!' One can imagine the atmosphere of confusion that prevails when the advocate has had no time to sort out his papers and put them all in order before the magistrate sits.

But the early bird can catch many worms. Defence advocates will be able to approach him with their suggestions: 'He'll have common assault if you'll drop the ABH'. 'I think he'd be prepared to plead to careless if you'll offer no evidence on the reckless.' You need time to consider whether such proposals are acceptable, and consistent with the demands of justice. In contested cases you can find out from the defence whether they intend to go for trial and if so what type of committal they want and the dates they wish to avoid, and, if there is no application for bail, you can ask the defending advocate if the defendant is prepared not to be produced for four weeks, if the case is going to take that long to prepare for the next stage of the proceedings. Above all you can see the gaoler before he gets too busy, and find out the order in which the cases are going to be called so that you can put your files in that order, for, make no mistake about it, the person who controls the list is the gaoler, and any advocate would be very unwise to get on bad terms with him.

As one who has always liked to remain in bed until the last possible minute, I am not sadistic enough to suggest that you should arrive at court at 8.30 if you have just one or two cases to deal with, but in that situation, like the defence advocate, you should certainly be there at least half an hour before the court is due to sit.

Otherwise, the general rules relating to advocacy which I have attempted to summarise at the end of the last chapter of this book apply. The prosecutor should be no less a good advocate than the defending barrister or solicitor. Some prosecutors seem so bowed down by the weight of the papers that they have had to carry into court that they are incapable of standing up straight when they address the Bench; this results in mumbling while fumbling. The abrupt advice to 'stand up, speak up, and then shut up' applies every bit as much to the representative of the Crown Prosecution Service as it does to the defence advocate. And do not let the burden of so much work affect the quality of the language you employ in court. Do not, please, reply as did one lady prosecutor appearing before me when I was complaining about a trial that had gone completely wrong: 'I'm sorry there's been such a cock-up in this case, but you must admit it's not as bad as some of the cock-ups we've had together'.

I had to retire from the Bench for a few minutes to contemplate in tranquillity this particular demonstration of 'Courtly English'!

14 Alpha and omega

In an earlier chapter I expressed my admiration of the dramatist Arthur Wing Pinero for his construction of the 'well-made play', by his habit of linking the end of his plays with their beginnings, and also reminding his audience in the final scene of sub-plots that had arisen earlier in the drama. May I therefore seek in this final chapter to remind my reader(s) of the reason for the delay in the first edition of this book seeing the light of day, namely that when I first had the idea of writing it more than twenty years ago Richard Du Cann produced *The Art of the Advocate* and when, a decade later, I felt that the market might have recovered from that highly successful onslaught upon it, Sir David Napley wrote *The Technique of Persuasion* which I was delighted and alarmed to see come out in a third edition. Then, just as I was about to complete my last chapter, a well-known barrister and Recorder named Keith Evans published *Advocacy at the Bar: a Beginner's Guide.* This book attracted a lot of publicity because in it Mr Evans alleged that 'a vast majority of them [English judges] favour the prosecution and lean against the defence', so that the difference between defending and prosecuting in a criminal case was, he said, like the difference between 'riding a bicycle uphill with the wind against you or downhill with the wind behind'. Now, I sometimes cycled to my court, so I was interested to see that the late Sir Melford Stevenson was reported in *The Times* as describing this suggestion of Mr Evans as 'bloody nonsense';—not exactly the 'Courtly English' which I commended in earlier chapters, but pretty pungent stuff which, coming from one of our more memorable judges of recent years, has probably ensured the book's commercial success, and might have discouraged me from continuing with my own work had I not got so far with it. Perhaps I should be grateful for the fact that when an Indian friend lent me his flat in Tobago there was an almost continuous rainstorm for a week that caused me *faute de mieux à faire* to settle down and write the first few chapters.

'Don't you find that the standard of advocacy among young barristers has deteriorated a lot since you and I were appearing before magistrates?' Crown Court judges and senior members of the Bar often ask me, for some reason hoping for the answer 'Yes'. In fact my answer is invariably: 'No, I think it has improved', and indeed it would be surprising if it were otherwise, bearing in mind the higher standard of entry into the profession, the greater emphasis on practical training (*pace* Keith Evans) the difficulty that all but the best have in finding a seat in Chambers, and the excellent filming classes which have been conducted on Saturdays by Mr Recorder Michael Hyams through which every Bar student has to pass. What has deteriorated, though, is the standard of manners. There is far more rudeness in court, as I opined in an earlier chapter. This, too, is inevitable, because the standard of manners in the country generally has gone down, and I don't think there are many schools nowadays which operate the syntactically incorrect motto 'Manners Maketh Man'. This, I think, is a pity, for good manners are not an exercise in hypocrisy (as some suspect) but do smooth the pathway to mutual understanding and happiness. Some advocates think it is clever to be abrasive in court: I regard them rather like children on 'activity bikes'. Being polite is not the same as being subservient, which is almost an unattractive as being rude. Uriah Heap would not have made a good advocate, anymore than one can admire the tactics of Sergeant Buzz-Fuzz. These ill manners often manifest themselves before the advocate gets up to address the court. Laughing and joking with other advocates, or discussing the case with the police officer before your case comes on but while the court is in session, is inconsiderate and selfish because it can distract the judge or magistrates from the task in hand, which may not matter to you but should be of great importance to them. Reading newspapers (even *The Times*!) in court looks casual and disrespectful. Usually your waiting time can best be employed by watching the current proceedings, studying the reactions of the judge or magistrates, but if the case before yours is unutterably boring—an old-style committal, for example—there is no reason why you should not work in court on that pleading or opinion for which your instructing solicitor has been pressing for the last fortnight. I always found this a very difficult thing to do—I find it hard to concentrate when something else is going on around me—so, as pleadings and opinions are important, have a copy of the *Weekly Law Reports* or *All England Reports* or the *Justice of the Peace* with you to read if what is going on in court becomes unbearably tedious and you cannot concentrate on your paper work. These little books of Reports are small enough for you to be able to read them and to turn over the pages without irritating the Bench. The advocate of today should take comfort from the fact that he is kept waiting far less than his predecessor of thirty years ago. When I was at the Bar it was not unusual to hang around a week at the Old Bailey or in the High Court before coming on. Judicial time was then regarded as the most precious commodity in the legal world. But recently I observed a new vice in counsel. Chewing gum! Defendants often do this, witnesses sometimes, police officers twice in my experience but—an advocate! With the chewing defendant I usually put the case back saying: 'I'm sorry to have disturbed your breakfast. I will deal with the case when you have had time to finish.' This usually had the desired effect, although one defendant nearly asphyxiated himself in his effort to dispose of the offending material and had to be revived by a glass of the rather stale water thoughtfully provided for my well-being.

What of the present standard of solicitors?

I think that we are very fortunate in the London courts in that there is a large team of (mainly young) solicitors appearing before us who are, for the most part, quite excellent. I do not know how we should cope if we had more long-winded or not very competent advocates. Most of our solicitors possess the most essential quality of the good advocate; they see the point and they get to it!

A good friend of mine is a very famous television personality. (He is, I hasten to add, the only very famous television personality that I know, but I will not quote his name as he is not a lawyer and it might cause him embarrassment. It would, however, be well-known to all my readers.) He had been stopped by the police for a minor motoring transgression, allegedly committed not far from where I live. The policeman, according to my friend (and I have no reason to disbelieve him), had behaved very badly. The officer clearly did not share the general public's (and my) opinion of my friend's star quality, was extremely rude as soon as he recognized him, and said that he would 'throw the book at him in court'. My friend came to see me and said that he wanted 'the best QC in London' to defend him in the magistrates' court. I think I could have managed this. Instead I said: 'I think I should arrange for you to have the services of the Solicitor-General'. 'The Solicitor-General!' my friend exclaimed, 'but surely he's a famous policitian.' 'No', I replied, 'I'm not suggesting that Sir Ian Percival should come to the magistrates' court for you. In each magistrates' court there seems to be one local solicitor who is outstandingly good. He is commonly known as the Solicitor-General of that Court. He will often do as good a job of advocacy as anyone can because he knows the court and has their ear and they know him and have learned to trust and respect him. The Solicitor-General of that Court often appears before me and is first-rate, and I know that he is well-liked there.' The solicitor concerned did the case, obtained a good result, and my famous friend was well-pleased with his first encounter with the courts—at about one-twentieth of the cost that he might have been called upon to pay for the services of 'the best QC in London', accompanied by his junior and the senior partner of the firm of instructing solicitors, and one or two of the staff who would have liked to be there to get his autograph.

The good 'Solicitor-General' is so good because he has the best opportunity of 'knowing his court'.

It is a regrettable possibility that the advocates of today are ruder because the judges are more polite. One advocate put it to me in this way: 'In your day and mine most of the judges were characters. They were lions, and they roared at us and we were afraid of them. Nowadays so many judges are colourless. They are so polite that the advocate can say anything to them and get away with it—especially with juries.' Bernard Levin, who favours faceless (and voiceless) judges, if he favours judges at all, would have been appalled by some of the giants of yesteryear. If the advocates are taking advantage just because the judges are now less formidable and fearsome, I think this is a pity. However, nothing that I say about being courteous should be construed as discouragement to the advocate to be courageous when the need arises—especially if he feels that a party to a case or a witness is being needlessly harassed by a judge or by the court. I observed a good example of such courage in a young barrister almost forty years ago on a Saturday afternoon at Lambeth Magistrates' Court. The magistrate was Geoffrey Rose, a fine old gentleman before whom it was always a joy to appear (even if one did realise that when he appeared to be taking notes he was, in fact, often making very skilful drawings of the advocates and parties appearing before him). It was a tragedy that Geoffrey Rose, the fairest of magistrates, should have died in office shortly after being harshly and publicly criticised for one of his decisions by the then Bishop of Southwark, Dr Mervyn Stockwood, who had not been in court when the decision was made. That case marked the beginning of the current trend of trial of the judiciary by newspaper. In that case the result appears to have been death.

On this Saturday afternoon the counsel concerned was defending in a case of common assault. The clerk concerned, who was a visitor to Lambeth that day, was very well known for his considerable knowledge of the law, the strict control that he liked to maintain over the court, his impatience (especially on Saturday afternoons) and the fact that he was very intolerant, especially with young solicitors and barristers. When counsel asked his second question in cross-examination the clerk turned round and demanded brusquely: 'What can possibly be the relevance of that question?'; to which the young counsel replied quietly and calmly: 'Relevancy is a matter for the learned magistrate and for me. Kindly do not interrupt again.'

I watched two things happen simultaneously. The clerk's bald head changed in colour to a bright shade of crimson, which it was to maintain for a surprisingly long time thereafter, and a faint smile of satisfaction came to the face of the magistrate, who then took out a red pencil with which he proceeded, I suspect, to draw what he could see of his clerk's head. There were no further interruptions, and Geoffrey Rose found for the defendant.

One of the most disturbing developments in the law in recent years has been the advent of the 'political lawyer'. When I was training for and in practice at the Bar the 'political lawyer' was unkown. Although we may all have had our various political persuasions, we never thought to take them into court with us. The lawyer was apolitical. Now, at the Bar, there are 'political Chambers', and 'Commonwealth Chambers' (for which the English members of the Bar are at least as much to blame as those Commonwealth members who are compelled to huddle together or not practise at all) and even a Society for Black Lawyers. There are firms of solicitors who are noted for their championing of Left-Wing or Right-Wing causes. There are even Law Centres which in property matters refuse to act for landlords and will espouse only the cases of tenants, though anyone who heard a radio programme in that very useful series called 'Checkpoint' about a wealthy Iranian student who had utterly terrorised an elderly couple, both old age pensioners, who had been misguided enough to let to him a room in their home (for which he never paid the rent), could be left in no doubt that exploitation can operate in more than one direction. The Iranian was represented by a Law Centre, whose representative persuaded the unfortunate landlords to pay the Iranian what for them was a substantial sum of money for alleged wrongful eviction when they had changed the locks against him to preserve their sanity—and perhaps their lives. All this is quite wrong. The former Vice-Chancellor Megarry often uses a phrase that I find inelegant, but which is certainly graphic and accurate, when he describes the barrister as 'the cabbie on the rank' (and counsel isn't entitled to stop after six miles either) whilst, dealing with the priority to be given to criminal work, where the liberty and reputation of the subject are at risk, Viscount Simon put it in this way, when addressing the Canadian Bar Association in Ottawa in 1943:

> 'There is an honourable tradition at the English Bar, that even a man who may be busy with many different cases, if he is called upon to defend the meanest criminal charged with the most despicable crime, is bound to give his own personal attention to that work, however odious and unremunerative it may be, to the exclusion of all other business coming his way, (for) such a helper is needed to make sure that the most is made of every flaw and of every gap in the net which seems to be closing round the unhappy man.'

So, twenty years or so after Lord Simon gave that address, I was a little surprised when, my having successfully appealed against a conviction of a member of the organisation that was the precursor of the National Front (and which was equally despicable, so that I am delighted to have forgotten its name) and my having got costs against the police prosecutor, a Jewish barrister who had been in court and had been a good friend for many, many years approached me to tell me that he was ashamed of me for what I had just achieved and that he would not speak to me again. Not long afterwards he very successfully defended in the 'Anarchist' trial—the first terrorist case in recent times—and I told him that I was surprised that he had become an anarchist. Having a sense of humour he saw the point, and we are now good friends again.

So the Bar should accept any case, however unpalatable or unrewarding. I am told that the Kray Twins expressed their gratitude to counsel who on legal aid fought so hard for them at the Old Bailey, saying that they had not really expected that anyone would want to take on their case at all. If this be so, there must have been some good in them, even if they did not understand the traditions of the Bar. I think that it is a pity that a film company should release a film about them at about the time of one of their own release from prison. If they want to make a 'fresh start' they will not have much of a chance, but no doubt the film will make a lot of money for the producer and distributors, who may not be too interested in justice and mercy. And I hope these high ideals apply to solicitors, too. It will be a sad day for civil liberties in this country when a person cannot walk into a solicitor's office and expect to be advised and represented without his political persuasions being questioned or influencing the conduct of his case.

Advocates who try to provoke the court with political pronouncements are about as fair as is Willie Hamilton with his constant attacks on the Queen, knowing that by tradition she has no right to reply; for the Bench must always appear—and be—apolitical. Political attacks on the Bench in court are rare. It has happened to me only once. A professor from the London School of Economics was accused of assaulting a policeman during a political demonstration. The policeman said he had done it. The professor said he hadn't. Both were good witnesses. I dismissed the case. The prosecutor was furious. Eyeing me with contempt, he said: 'You may like to know that this particular defendant has two previous convictions arising from his activities at demonstrations'. I replied: 'I think that is irrelevant and grossly improper'. He said: 'Well, I thought you ought to know, as you are notoriously liberal in your views'. As the words were spoken, I cannot say whether or not 'liberal' was supposed to have a capital 'L'.

The balance was to be restored not long afterwards when my attention was drawn to an article in an underground magazine which referred to me as 'traditionalist' and 'reactionary' on account of my attitude to those who trade in drugs. The magazine was right to the extent that this is a group of people who do not command my immediate sympathy. And I was quite flattered to learn that I had been attacked in a Madrid underground magazine for my alleged attitude to drug-pushers.

But I was astonished when, in 1983, the Dean of the Council of Legal Education called my attention to an anonymous letter in the second issue of *Bar News* suggesting that I had affinities with the National Front. In reality, I believe that nobody apart from my family and closest friends has any idea of what my political views are, and that is the way it should be. The Bench, like the advocate, must be completely apolitical. (It is true that I have earlier on referred to the National Front as 'despicable' but that is because I do not regard the National Front as a political party but as a disease, and I say the same of their opposite numbers at the other end of the political spectrum. They are about as useful to our free society as gnats and wasps.) Political utterances to or in or about the court are not worth making or listening to, because they invariably come from extremists whose inappropriate diatribes are worthless when put into the Scales of Justice. Keep politics out of court!

What should be done, you may ask, when you are briefed by a political faction in a particular cause? Then use the whole weight of your *legal* argument and the power of your advocacy to bring about the result that those you represent desire. But do not yourself be hauled into the political arena. The advocate does not have to repeat everything that his client instructs him to say. There are many occasions on which discretion is the better part of valour. To take a mundane example, your client contesting a charge of burglary instructs you: 'Tell them I've always put my hand up before and I wouldn't have got involved in this just after coming out of a three year stretch'. In most—but not necessarily all—cases, this would be better left unsaid. Remember that as advocate you are a filter, not a mouthpiece.

A barrister whose Christian name is William was appearing some years ago before an Old Bailey judge with whom he was not very popular, and the judge was getting irritated not only by the barrister's verbosity but also by his instructing solicitor's irksome habit of pulling counsel's gown to give him little notes which the barrister felt obliged to read and digest before proceeding further with his lengthy final speech to the jury. (This is a most aggravating habit on the part of some solicitors, which can result in an appreciable increase in the sale of aspirin and like products to counsel. I once saw an eminent barrister strike a solicitor, who was constantly indulging in this annoying practice, over the head with a heavy legal tome—to the obvious delight of the trial judge—but this is not a custom that I would recommend to the young counsel keen to increase his practice at the Bar.) Eventually the Old Bailey judge could stand it no longer and, ignoring legal privilege, he commented: 'I'm sure the jury would be very interested to know what was in that last note, produced at such a late stage in the proceedings'. 'Oh, just a billet doux, my Lord', replied counsel airily. 'Are you sure it wasn't a Billy Don't?' enquired the judge.

In deference to that great and witty judge, Alan King Hamilton, may I summarise what I have attempted to say in these fourteen chapters on the rôle of the advocate, with six 'Billy Do's' and six 'Billy Don'ts'?

The DOs

(1) DO prepare your case three times over, including from the standpoint of the other side.
(2) DO be honest with the court.
(3) DO try to help the court to reach a just conclusion.
(4) DO care and show that you care without becoming emotional.
(5) DO be courteous to everyone in court.
(6) DO be prepared to stand up for what you know is right.

The DON'Ts

(1) DON'T be late.
(2) DON'T be a bully.

(3) DON'T be pompous.
(4) DON'T be political.
(5) DON'T dwell on the obvious (eg burden of proof, presumption in favour of bail).
(6) DON'T ask too many questions in cross-examination.

And of course don't go on so long that you bore those who have to listen to you. In the hope that I have not done the equivalent of this, I thank any reader(s) who has/have had the patience and stamina to remain with me until

THE END

Index